DESIGN A LIFE THAT WORKS

Oct 7, 2006

To my friend Connie —
I hope this book aids you
as you grow your seed of
leadership and Design A Life
that works.

Mike

D1411646

DESIGN A LIFE THAT WORKS

ON THE SAME PAGE PLANNER™

The Rivendell Book Factory

This book is dedicated to all the important people in our lives.

Distributed to the trade by
Cardinal Publishers Group
2222 Hillside Avenue, Suite 100
Indianapolis, Indiana 46218
(800) 296-0481

Produced by
The Rivendell Book Factory
ISBN 0-944353-16-9

Art & Illustration: Chris Green of HKW Associates
Book Design & Production: Bill Segrest of HKW Associates
HKW Associates • Architecture, Interiors, Graphics
www.HKW.com

Author Appearances & Press Inquiries
Please contact: Greg Womble Communications
Greg@WomCom.net

Grateful acknowledgement is given to the Center for Creative Leadership,
with campuses in Greensboro, Colorado Springs, San Diego, Brussels and
Singapore, for their kind permission to reprint research data from a 1999
Benchmarks® study, "Lessons of a Diverse Workforce," a continuation of their
earlier landmark Benchmarks® research, "Lessons of Experience." CCL® and
Benchmarks® are registered trademarks owned by the
Center for Creative Leadership, www.ccl.org.

The author especially wishes to offer thanks to Dr. William E. Hull for his
generous permission to reprint a key paragraph from his work *The Four-Way
Test: Core Values of the Rotary Movement*. Dr. Hull's sincere belief that to resolve
conflicts in a modern, pluralistic society we must first accept and acknowledge
*that the best place to begin a dialogue is not by discussing our conflicting answers,
but rather to agree on what are the right questions*
is foundational to this work.

A Limited Edition of 3,000 copies
Printed and bound in Nashville, Tennessee, by Vaughan Printing

TABLE OF CONTENTS

Preface   Your Working Journal

Introduction   Laying the Foundation for Change

1 • Values & Vision   Be Somebody

2 • Career Mission   A Peaceful Career

3 • Assumptions   The Keys I Haven't Lost Yet

4 • Stakeholders   Bridges to Secure

5 • Objectives   CEOs & EKGs

6 • S.W.O.T.   The Examined Life

7 • Key Decisions   Weighting and Waiting

8 • Action Plan   Henry's Awful Mistake

Afterword   Why Faith and God Matter

Appendix   Additional Resources

WORKING JOURNAL

Preface

*The plans of the diligent lead to profit
as surely as haste leads to poverty*

Proverbs 21:5

The purpose of this preface is to establish the premise and clarify the logic on how this working journal can be used to create your one-page life plan.

VANTAGE POINT

Rest assured, every leader experiences the pain of discipline or the pain of regret.

Randy Sain, engineer

Our goals can only be reached through the vehicle of a plan, in which we must fervently believe, and upon which we must vigorously act. There is no other route to success.

Pablo Picasso, artist

Aim at heaven and you will get earth "thrown in."
Aim at earth and you'll get neither.

C.S. Lewis, author

THE SMARTEST MAN IN THE WORLD

Sleet and driving rain pelted the windshield of a small twin-engine airplane as a nasty thunderstorm tossed it about like a ping pong ball in the night sky. Inside the plane sat a Boy Scout, a pastor, a famous computer guru, and, of course, the pilot.

Suddenly, a bolt of lightning cracked and, as these things so often happen, the left engine sputtered ... and came back to life again. A moment later, it sputtered again ... but this time it died.

Panic gripped the four passengers as they frantically began a search for emergency equipment, preparing for the worst. To their horror they found only three parachutes.

Although one engine was still running, the pilot shot up from her seat and said, "Guys, I have four children and a husband. They need me." Then she reached down and grabbed a parachute. "The plane is set to 'auto-pilot.' It's a good bet you'll make it to the nearest airport." She strapped on the parachute, yelling over the noise of the wind and the remaining engine, "Good luck, I'm outta here."

The technology wizard immediately turned to the pastor and the Boy Scout and said, "Fellows, I am one of the smartest men in the world. I have created a new computer program that is going to revolutionize commerce as we know it. I, too, must go. Business can't possibly progress without my ideas; I am so sorry." He then leaned over to snatch up a parachute and jumped out of the airplane.

Although the wind continued to roar as the two hapless passengers stared out the plane's darkened doorway, an eerie calm descended in the cabin. With great compassion and a practiced control, the pastor slowly turned to the boy and said, "Son, I have lived a long and faithful life. I have no concern at all about …."

The Scout broke in, a thin, wry smile lighting up his face, "… No problem, Reverend, the smartest man in the world just picked up my backpack and jumped out of the airplane."

The premise of this, your working journal, is that smart
people know that success is not determined by how
smart they are—it is determined by the decisions they make.

VANTAGE POINT

ACT QUICKLY ... NOT TOO QUICKLY

Some people may say I am a quail hunter. But, in fact, when asked, I prefer to tell them I am a bird dog owner. Without doubt I enjoy hunting; but what I actually care for more than quail, pheasant, or grouse on the family table is the time I get to spend with my bird dog, Annie.

Most every hunting dog will, by nature, flush out and chase any quarry they sense in the woods or in the wilds. This bark-and-get-at-'em approach works well for most. A dog's natural disposition to scare up and set chase is easily managed, and when a dog is properly rewarded by his handler this will lead to many successful hunts and a full larder.

But bird dogs do just the opposite of what nature instructs virtually every other dog to do. When a well-trained bird dog, like my English setter Annie, hits the scent, she has been instructed to freeze, to slow down and focus on what's truly important. She becomes still, absolutely silent, content in her role as servant to others. Holding the covey of birds, she stands at the ready, hyper-alert, absolutely in tune with her surroundings.

I have experienced a bird dog holding point for so long that he finally fell to the ground from sheer exhaustion, legs having given out, still pointing. It becomes the bird dog's purpose in life to find and hold birds for its master. A clear, steady purpose. A purpose my Annie carries with great dignity.

As you use this book to generate ideas to help you get a clearer picture of your life dreams and career aspirations, you will sense when you are getting close to what you really want out of life. When you come to a page with only one sentence on it, take the opportunity to stop and be still. When you read a short story or face a question you may have never considered, when you sense you are closing in on an idea in tune with your needs, reach deep inside, be still … and stay on point.

Theologian and teacher Glenn Clark helps to frame this concept, stating, "I believe all creative power comes from great stillness. If then, we just quiet and afterwards act, the action will go further for there is alignment. We should not have to do much to change the whole world."

The life-strategy process in this book, like a good bird dog, perhaps, may open up a clearing for you to be still and to know. Give yourself permission to listen, to look at life from a different vantage point.

An effective strategic decision-making discipline requires one to
slow down long enough to hear the hard truths about oneself, to
focus on the things that really matter.

VANTAGE POINT

VALUES & VISION
CAREER MISSION

ASSUMPTIONS
STAKEHOLDERS

OBJECTIVES
S.W.O.T.

KEY DECISIONS

ACTION PLAN

SMART TRANSITIONS BEGIN WITH A PLAN

I have analyzed and defined five key personality traits and tendencies of the people who are most likely to benefit from the planning process presented in the organization of this book. The reliability of this assessment of personality traits has held true regardless of a person's current economic situation, education, or rung on the ladder of recognition.

> **S** uccess-driven workaholic who thrives on information
> **M** easures self in a rational and objective manner
> **A** ccepts fact that leadership growth requires a spiritual center.
> **R** emains in control at all times, if at all possible
> **T** rusts that transition and change are opportunities for growth

In my practice, I have found that smart people in transition naturally gravitate to any deliberative process that promises to slow them down enough to help them develop a clear perspective for making positive changes in their life. My solution is to organize the chapters in this book to track a logical sequence of priorities.

Values & Vision	Define your reason for being and the logic to your life.
Career Mission	Develop confidence about your future work.
Assumptions	Frame a concise statement of your management style.
Stakeholders	Identify those for whom you build bridges and why.
Objectives	Set measurable & time-sensitive priorities.
S.W.O.T.	Analyze the hard truths about your current situation.
Key Decisions	Clarify the decisions to focus on for the next year.
Action Plan	Avoid Henry's awful mistake.

The result is a flexible-yet-controlled interactive environment—what I believe to be a unique, compelling experience—where you will be encouraged to inquire into the facts and nature of your current situation … moving forward with deliberate speed towards the transition you will make.

I sincerely thank you for deciding to invest your time and money in the thoughts and words of an author and business coach who has learned the hard and slow way that … if you don't design your life, someone who thinks they're smarter than you will design it for you.

So, for Heaven's sake, design a life that works. It's time.

Michael Alan Tate

LAYING THE FOUNDATION FOR CHANGE

Introduction

A generous man will prosper; he who refreshes others will himself be refreshed.

Proverbs, 11:25

The purpose of this introduction is to help you set the
foundation on which you can build a meaningful
and actionable life plan.

VANTAGE POINT

A problem well stated is a problem half solved.

Charles F. Kettering, engineer

There is a wonderful, mythical law of nature that the three things we crave most in life—happiness, freedom, and peace of mind—are always attained by giving them to someone else.

Peyton Conway March, soldier

Our remedies oft in ourselves do lie.

William Shakespeare, playwright

In this introductory task, *Laying the Foundation for Change,* you will address two questions.

1. Why is this a good time to develop your life plan?

2. How prepared are you to move to the next level?

VANTAGE POINT

RIGHT TIME, NEXT LEVEL

The country porch rocking chairs were active that rainy morning at the B&B in the Ozarks. A group of uptown bikers had rendezvoused at the Inn to begin their motorcycle caravan to the Grand Canyon. All the bikers had left the old wooden porch to prepare for the road, except for a middle-aged lady, an educational testing specialist, and her neurosurgeon-biker husband. An interesting couple.

She explained to me, "We are both leaders in our professions, high-profile workaholics with urgent things to do. We always believed we could only afford to take a few days off or the world would stop ..." She hesitated, a faraway look in her eyes. "This is the first time we've ever taken a two-week vacation. We've had some things happen recently that have made us rethink our lives."

One of my mentors, the late Bill McGrane, Sr., was a master teacher, always full of questions and loaded with wisdom. One of the many "McGraneisms" I will always remember is his view on personal change: "Mike, the simple reality is that people change for one of two reasons. One, it's the in-thing to do, or, two, a significant emotional event occurs."

My experience has taught me that smart people don't change because it's trendy or the socially acceptable thing to do. They rethink, change, and move to the next level because something significant has happened or is realistically anticipated to happen in their life or their career.

Isn't the "next level" something we all aspire to at some point or other in our lives? When smart people finally realize it's time, they inevitably begin to look back to see how they got to where they are; they test the assumptions and objectives that brought them to the pass they now face; they analyze their current strengths and weaknesses; they question the motives and actions behind the bridges they've built and the values they've established. In short, smart people understand that before they make their next transition, voluntary or involuntary, they still have work to do.

For the motorcycle couple—the testing specialist and the neurosurgeon—the "right time" was when they realized the world wouldn't stop if they held off from work for a few days; the "next level" just happened to be the front porch of an inn in Arkansas. Is this the right time for you to make your transition, and are you prepared to do it right?

NO TIME LIKE THE PRESENT

A proud young man, who for all outward signs appeared to be the picture of assuredness and confidence, felt like he was wandering through life. This smart young man had the good judgment to summon up his courage and tell his friend and mentor that even though he had a general direction in mind, he still felt crippled, defeated by a lack of clarity. With support and encouragement, however, he concluded it was time … time to finally create a strategy for his life.

But he had no idea where or how to begin. Once again, he approached his friend and mentor for advice. A tape based on a bestselling self-help book of the day was the recommendation. On a quiet drive in the country, the young man listened to the tape as the author posed a series of questions like "How would you describe your perfect day" or "What drains your energy?" or "What would you do with your career if you didn't need money to do it?" The young man was so intrigued he regularly pulled off the road and sat in the car to write his answer to each one.

By the end of the day he had created a picture of his ideal work objectives. He had added a few target dates, had thought through how he would begin working towards them, and, as a result, he successfully created his first "life strategy." Ten pages long; unwieldy, perhaps, and difficult to get through, it at least was a plan that made sense to him.

Having clear direction in a written form paid big dividends for the young man over the next 10 years. I say this with great conviction because I was that young man. I took a job in corporate outplacement, helping executives and professionals get back on course, finding the jobs that they truly loved. I shared my evolving understanding of the "life strategy" process with my diverse client base, helping each to put the contents of their personal process together in a 3-ring binder with tabs.

I soon discovered, however, that no one ever looks at a plan in a 3-ring binder more than twice … unless, perhaps, they are physically threatened in some way! Yes, the life-strategy process did work, but the product, and the *organization* of the end result, needed to be simplified so that people would put their plans to work. For productive people, less time means greater value.

So, planning by the pound is rather foolish, and that young man, who happens to be me, asked a question that would very shortly change his life: Is there a simpler way to engineer an actionable plan?

For productive people, the less time spent
on a task, successfully completed, yields
the greatest value to the job.

VANTAGE POINT

CONCISE PLANS LEAD TO ACTION

In the mid 1990s, I joined Vantage Associates, a management consulting firm that specializes in strategic planning projects with senior level teams. At Vantage Associates, our planning philosophy, techniques, and key questions are based on more than 25 years of experience in helping organizations create road maps to their desired future. This same philosophy and methodology has helped countless individuals think more clearly and strategically about how to move their career and personal lives to a more fulfilling and productive level.

When I first began with Vantage Associates, my job was to work with the leaders of these teams, guiding them to design leadership development plans to support their goals and their organizations' business initiatives. My audience may have changed but I still faced the inevitable conflict between the broad scope of the process and the need for a simplified statement of results—in a world where binders of 100+ pages remained the norm!

Meanwhile, my business partners had developed a way to summarize multi-year strategic business planning projects onto one sheet of paper. As the ancient saying goes, "The ox you are looking for, you might be sitting on top of." The answer I was seeking for a functional, easy-to-use personal life-strategy was right there, but it took another insight to bring it to light.

The genesis for the ON THE SAME PAGE PLANNER™ (sample plans are found between each chapter and a planner template is printed on the inside of the dust jacket for your convenience) occurred in 1996. My business partner had just completed an annual strategic plan update for a small, privately held company. The organization's entire plan had been condensed to one side of an 8 ½ X 11 page. As the meeting closed, with the one-page plan in hand, the CEO turned to the executive group and said casually, "Now that we have our company plan on one side of this page, what would it take for each of you to write your personal strategic plan on the other side of the page?"

I could not have anticipated how this CEO's off-the-cuff request to his staff would yield truly extraordinary results. Since that time, his family business began trading on the New York Stock Exchange and today is a leading player in national real-estate markets. For my part, I took his request to heart and over the ensuing years refined this simple but powerful business and life alignment process. It became the cornerstone of my thriving consulting practice in leader development.

As seventeenth century scholar and cleric,
Baltasar Gracian, once reminded us,
"Good things, when short, are twice as good."

VANTAGE POINT

IT'S TIME. ARE YOU READY?

A number of years ago, I woke up in the middle of the night thinking about my work. A person I was coaching was having particular trouble moving his team forward. He said all the right things, had all the right technical knowledge and experience but his team wasn't achieving key business initiatives. Trying to make sense of that situation, asking myself what was missing. What was it about this guy that was causing this stalemate with his team to happen?

A key skill of any successful leader is the ability to coach and mentor people. This guy couldn't coach. He had drive and determination. He had read all the "how-to" coaching books and knew the right words, but he was missing the key underlying, foundational attribute of all truly successful leaders. He was missing a spirit of generosity.

Robert Hargrove, in *Masterful Coaching*, explains it this way,

Coaching is a way of being, not just a technique that allows you to help other people achieve success. Generosity of spirit allows you to give people the gift of your presence in any conversation. It motivates you to give authentic feedback that helps someone grow and learn, as well as give praise that affirms that person. People with generosity of spirit give others credit.

Before I fell back to sleep that night, I wrote on a pad eight words: Give Thanks, Give Credit, Give Back, and Give Up. Those were the variations on the concepts behind Hargrove's generosity of spirit that I'd seen over and over in truly successful people. These traits were definitely lacking in that executive I was working with. It was from that series of events that what I now call "The Give Factors" came into being—

Give Thanks ...	For what you are most grateful for at this time
Give Credit ...	To those most responsible for your success, helping you and being there for you
Give Back ...	With greater frequency in a selfless way
Give Up ...	Or let go of something intentionally to reach a new level of success

In my experience as an executive consultant, a person's response to these Give Factors reveals a certain depth of character found in those who are ready to take the next step in becoming high performance leaders in business and life. Ask yourself whether you are a giver or a taker, and you will know if you are ready for the next level.

The former president of the Republic of South Africa and a Nobel Peace Prize laureate once said, "I have discovered the secret that after climbing a great hill one finds many more to hills to climb. I have taken a moment to rest, to steal a view of the glorious vista that surrounds me, to look at the distance I have come. But I can rest only for a moment, for with my freedom comes responsibilities, and I dare not linger, for my walk is not yet ended."

VANTAGE POINT

WHAT DO YOU GIVE THANKS FOR?

❑ In Your Life

❑ In Your Career

❑ In General

TO WHOM DO YOU GIVE CREDIT FOR SUCCESS?

People who cause you to look at your own direction. They ☐ force you to face important questions about your own life.

People who advise you ☐ and encourage you. People who just listen.

People who are fundamental to getting ☐ your day-to-day work done.

Highly acclaimed people you aspire to emulate ☐ and from whose lives you intend to learn.

HOW HAVE YOU GIVEN BACK IN A SELFLESS WAY?

❏ Business

❏ Organization

❏ Career

❏ Family

❏ Faith

❏ Community

WHAT HAVE YOU GIVEN UP TO REACH THIS MOMENT?

What career strategy that made you successful in ☐
the past did you decide to let go of, a decision that now
allows you to focus your energy and time differently
and now enables you to move on to the next level?

What life strategy, beliefs or assumptions did you ☐
give up over the years in order to move closer to
who you are meant to be?

Who did you forgive that allowed you to move forward? ☐

A FEW MOMENTS & A HEAP OF THANKS

My wife, Patricia, who lives a life of unshakable faith, constant prayer, joyful music, and service.

My father, Odus, who stands for what he believes and trusts God in all things. He taught me that a good name is better than great riches and to leave a note when you leave the house. My appropriately-named mother, Constance, who lives in selfless (and often secret) service to others. Besides teaching me how to shoot a BB gun, she taught me the true meaning of giving back to others, especially those who can never pay you back.

My sons, Brad, for the writing skills he applied to this book and his unwavering belief in this old man's ideas, and, Brandon, who told me five years ago to write this book and who did the Web site design.

My sister, Gloria, the smart one in the family and the kindest person I know. My brother, Larry, the biggest-hearted person I know, who reminds me to always treat my family as I treat my best customers. Pete, my bother-in-law, who reminds me that life's short—make it an adventure.

Phil Ronniger, who went the second mile for a guy with a dream and taught me to trust my inner voice in order to help others find theirs. Elizabeth Jefferies, my model of professionalism in the business of speaking, who taught me that clients most value what we believe not just what we know. Jim Marshall, who taught me to "stay in the pocket" and that God always sends the perfect number of people at the right time. He taught me how to sell. Cliff Eslinger, my friend, mentor, coach, and the executive consultant who made up, passed along, and actually prays, as I do now, "the consultants prayer." Richard Bolles, whose generosity of spirit made a way for me to experience his exceptional knowledge and wisdom in the art and science of career advising. His only request for payment for his time was to "give it away," to pass it on.

To all my friends, my clients, and executive teams who took a chance on me by letting me create and implement some unorthodox but nonetheless compelling experiences ... and who still call me back!

SERVICE ABOVE SELF

I was inducted into Rotary International 14 years ago. Rotary is the oldest and, by most measures, the most effective and influential civic organization in the world. Over the past 101 years, Rotary has raised funds and created the largest civic philanthropic foundation in the world. As an organization, we have over 3 million members in 31 countries.

Rotary's goal is to promote ethics in business and peace in the world. One of the many objectives soon to be achieved is the eradication of polio in the world. I still marvel at the success of this volunteer group. How has Rotary done so much for so many people worldwide? What is the secret?

The secret is that the organizational vision is founded on the core value: "Service above self." Underlying this value is the real power of Rotary: it's individual members' shared commitment to a simple criteria for living and working each day, as expressed in what is called The Four-Way Test:

Of the things we think, say, and do we will ask ourselves—
        Is it the truth?
        Is it fair to all concerned?
        Will it build goodwill and better friendships?
        Will it be beneficial to all concerned?

Dr. William E. Hull, in *The Four-Way Test—Core Values of the Rotary Movement*, states, "The Four-Way test does not decree how we are to honor these four criteria but only puts them in the form of questions which we must answer for ourselves. In the pluralistic world of the twenty-first century, differences run so deep that the best place to begin a dialogue is not by discussing our conflicting answers, but rather to agree on what are the right questions."

My hope is that this working journal will help you as you seek to ask the right questions. My belief is that once you begin the process of engineering your life—a life that works—you will be reinvigorated and emboldened to continue your challenge of making the world a better place.

1. WHY IS IT TIME FOR YOUR LIFE PLAN?

❑ Does your motivation have to do with your business, your career, your family, or your faith or a combination of these?

❑ Could this be a good time simply because you were given this book by someone you respect and admire and it seems easy and quick enough to accomplish ... low risk of disappointment and you will honor the friend who gave it to you ... everybody wins, whatever the outcome?

❑ Has something significant happened to make you rethink how you will live you life?

2. HOW PREPARED ARE YOU?

NO DUMMIES ALLOWED

This book is written for experienced leaders who want to sharpen their focus and simplify their path to success. This is not a guide for idiots or a life's little instruction book. The truth is that it takes a smart person to know that "success" cannot be absolutely defined, that success is plain and simply "a life that works." This working journal is here to help you—

> **Create context, not content.**
> **Isolate a "Vantage Point" from multiple "points of view."**
> **Ask good questions and get even better answers.**

You see, my clients have told me that what they really want is not more content, but rather more context. They each want to take their many years of experience—a treasure of hard-won information—and put it to work. They want their highly individualized knowledge base to inform and enrich their lives. They want out of the data smog and into a personalized working strategy, a design for their future.

My promise to you is that in a short period of time—in less time than you thought possible—this working journal's accessible, interactive content will lead you to harness the power found in the context of your own life. The result will be based on the resolution of your personal values and your belief systems rooted in lessons learned from experience.

I've found that smart people often will say they want stability in their lives, but at the same time they will fiercely resist this natural desire for stable viewpoints. This working journal, however, requires one to do so. Chapters will include stories, thought triggers, and fast track exercises to expedite your practical progress as you design your life plan. The appendix will suggest you visit my Web site—OnTheSamePg.com (password is *yourway*)—where you will find collateral resources and reference material, including "asking for feedback" forms and helpful planning templates.

All chapters open with two questions, which when answered, will shift you from an internal point of view to an external vantage point. Rather than looking at a core problem from the inside out, you will begin to look at the problem from the outside in.

The true purpose of any planning episode is to compel you to ask good questions in order that you will get better answers … answers that adequately reflect your own distinctive definition of success.

WHAT IS IT ABOUT SAM?

Sam is a lucky man and a great leader. He knows the two things that matter the most in business—1) What he wants, and 2) A really good question.

When Sam called me to help him, his team was not in trouble; as a matter of fact, his division had led the company in production and profits for many years. When I asked him how he had accomplished this, without the slightest hesitation or posturing, he gave a little credit to "the luck of the draw" on his part but the lion's share of the effort's success he attributed to the great work of the people on his team. Now Sam wanted to make the team even better.

In a few bullet points, he had clarified what he wanted for the future of the team and the organization. The next words out of his mouth made it clear that he not only knew but was also very much at home with the need for asking really good questions. "Over the last few months," he said, "I have been asking myself what is it about me that is keeping this team from moving to the next level?"

What is it about me? This just may be the best question of all really good questions. Put forward, in different words from different angles, by philosophers, poets, and prophets, found in prayers, speeches, and books since civilization began, it is perhaps the one indispensable question necessary for progress and growth and the advancement of civilization.

In many ancient tribal cultures the warriors, the leaders of the tribe, are said to have strived to walk as if every step were a prayer. I have yet to learn what those prayers might have actually been or if this only figuratively represented a posture of humility and gratitude. But I believe if there were such a prayer, "a walking prayer," and that there was a warrior who did indeed pray this prayer on his road to leadership, it might have gone something like the following—an executive-summary, modern reworking of the *Serenity Prayer*:

> God, grant me the serenity to accept the people I cannot change, the courage to change the one I can, and the wisdom to know it is me.

So, what is it about Sam? We've learned that it really isn't about Sam ... or anyone else around us for that matter ... the really good question to ask just before we set out on the road to any new enterprise is ... *What is it about me?*

VALUES & VISION
CAREER MISSION

ASSUMPTIONS
STAKEHOLDERS

OBJECTIVES
S.W.O.T.

KEY DECISIONS

ACTION PLAN

VALUES & VISION

1 • Be Somebody

The purpose of this chapter, *Values & Vision*, is to gain a clearer picture of your reason for being and the logic to your life.

VANTAGE POINT

*I always wanted to be somebody. I guess
I should have been more specific.*

Lily Tomlin, comedienne

*Anything that transcends eating, drinking, and making
money must begin with a leap of faith.*

Sam Keen, philosopher

I'd kill for a Nobel Peace Prize.
World Leader, little-known

In this first step, *Be Somebody*, you will address two dispositive questions.

1.   What are your personal, spiritual values?

2.   What is your corporate, community vision?

VANTAGE POINT

WHAT WOULD IT BE WORTH?

A successful-looking business man attended a mountaintop retreat. He did so partly because he was tapped as high-potential by higher-ups, and partly because he wanted to get away from the thickening data smog and endless buzz of daily business problems. Secretly, he hoped to recapture the feeling of fulfillment, even enthusiasm, in his life and career, but …

His energy was soon evaporated by the endless litany of insights, observations, and suggestions coming from his feedback team. Far too many hours had slipped away mulling over peer reviews, white papers, and 360-degree data. Half a dozen personal assessment instruments were stacked behind colored tabs and countless Ivy League MBA articles bulged out of the "To-Be-Read" section of his top-grain leather binder.

Near the end of the week the executive, discouraged and data-burdened, took a walk in the woods and unknowingly wandered into an adjoining military installation. A young soldier, standing guard at the perimeter, shouted, "Halt. Who are you and why are you here?" The executive perked up and asked, "What did you say?" The solider became even more stern and repeated, "Who are you and why are you here?" The executive asked, "How much do you get paid?" The solider, caught off guard by the question, said, "Why does that matter to you?" "Because," the executive replied, "I'll pay you twice what you make to come to my office and ask me those same two questions every day."

An attorney recently used the word "dispositive," a word I had never heard, so I looked it up in a dictionary and found, to my surprise, that it wasn't there. Now, a lawyer is, by stock and trade, a wordsmith, and I was certain my friend would not use a word if it didn't have a citation somewhere in the annals of English law or literature. Sure enough, a trip to the Oxford English Dictionary led me to the following: "having the characteristic of dealing with a thing definitively and with finality."

"Values" are strongly held principles or convictions that are formulated over the course of a lifetime. Ideally, one's values will guide action and dictate behavior in all life situations, and, as such, values lie at the heart of one's good name. "Vision" describes our hopes, our dreams of how the world can be different simply because we are here. Our vision embodies a noble cause far beyond our unique capabilities and strengths to attain alone. We need others to have a vision. Since our values comprise who we are and our vision denotes our purpose in life, let's begin by asking ourselves, is it possible to "dispositively" define these two elements in our lives?

A LIFE TRUE TO PLUMB

My father is a master carpenter, always in pursuit of excellence. When I was a young boy, he often included me on some his favorite projects. One of my fondest memories was when he would pull what most tradesmen call the "plumb bob" out of an old, beaten up, immensely beautiful and—to my childhood imagination—wonderfully mysterious tool box.

The plumb bob consists of a lead-weighted cone (a "bob") attached to a length of string (the "line"). This simple devise employs the law of gravity to insure perfect level and vertical alignment. I can still picture the satisfied look of my father with the line in his hand, whispering "This is good" as he stood straight and tall by a wall built perfectly true to plumb.

My father's close and dear friend Reverend Ralph Clark was my boyhood pastor. During his forty-plus years in the ministry, he led several congregations in our area. A few years ago, he called and asked if I would speak at his funeral. I was honored and accepted under one condition, "that he give me ten years to prepare." Three weeks later he died.

At the viewing I sat with his son, Tommy, a life-long friend of mine. We talked about the service. I asked him what he wanted me to say about his father. He said he wanted a celebration of who he was and what he stood for, his legacy revealed to all. Over 500 people attended the funeral service. I stood up and made a few remarks about what this pastor had meant to the communities he served.

I then stopped and asked each person to think about Pastor Clark, what he stood for and how he had impacted their lives. I then asked each person gathered there to put those thoughts into a few words by whispering them to the people sitting next to them, on both sides. The result may have sounded like a mumbled din to some, but in reality it was the beautiful music of a life, a life of values that had been lived right—values shared and remembered.

Our life values are like the weighted cone at the end of life's plumb line, like whispers gathered into music. Imagine this line, these whispers offering you the necessary information to assist you as you make the determination if you are living true to yourself and your creator. Define your values, and your vision will follow on its heels.

What values do you hope the children in your life will
follow in the years ahead and what words
do you hope they will whisper at your funeral?

VANTAGE POINT

WORKS IN LIFE, WORKS IN BUSINESS

Although we all have core values that guide our personal decisions, we recognize there is no simple checklist to live by or choose from. Most religions have a creed or statement of values, and since many of us grew up in a religion, we often choose to keep the religious values of our childhood. Others without religious background choose to establish values from a humanitarian or an atheistic perspective.

However one may have developed their core values, smart people inevitably reach a point where they are no longer willing to stake their lives on the values they have "learned." They demand authenticity. They want to take ownership in the tenets of their beliefs, and they are willing to test their values, to challenge them in order to make them theirs in truth.

Values result from core beliefs, and only you can decide if they are authentic. What is important is that the values you adopt and nurture are clear and strong. We live according to what we believe, and our life is a unique expression of that belief. Over a lifetime, your constant values sharpened and focused by intelligent challenge will result in your life's vision.

Most of us are aware of individuals whose lives don't work because they are based on changing desires, thoughts, and feelings instead of strongly held beliefs. The drive to be liked or accepted is a common trait of many a struggling manager. These people are driven and controlled by their weak egos and insecurities rather than drawn to a set of values. Who among us wants to be labeled "a person of convictions based on his last conversation?"

Jim Collins and Jerry Porras wrote a classic article in the Harvard business review entitled, "Building Your Company's Vision." The authors argue that companies which enjoy multi-generational success can be shown to have clearly defined core values and a core purpose that remains fixed ... while their business strategies and practices endlessly adapt to a changing world.

A group of managers from one of these leading companies was asked what they would do if the market changed and their values didn't matter to their customers anymore. What if their customers told them that the only thing that mattered was speed and cost? They answered, "Our vision is very important to us and always will be, no matter what. If our current markets don't value it, we will find markets that do." And thus the world can be made better. Perhaps, just perhaps, the potential for such progressive good is why we're here?

A young skater told himself that if he won a gold medal at the
Winter Olympics he would use the opportunity to speak to the
world about something important to him. His fifteen minutes,
he said, would be put to good use. He won the gold and the
interview was held, and he quickly turned the world's attention
to those suffering in Africa. Now, imagine you have been given
a similar platform on which you can speak to the world and you
only have time for one thing to say. What would you say?

VANTAGE POINT

A few companies' corporate vision statements ...

- Improve the standard of living around the world.—Cargill
- Preserve and improve human life.—Merck
- Make people happy.—Walt Disney Corporation
- Give unlimited opportunity to women.—Mary Kay

A few individuals' community vision statements ...

- A country where what we have is more important than what I have
- Accessibility to healthcare worldwide
- Compassionate stewardship
- A world that exemplifies God's joy and compassion
- Most profitable small business enterprises in the world
- A world free of racism
- Justice for the disadvantaged
- A world that has learned to laugh at itself

VANTAGE POINT

LEADERSHIP BEGINS WITH SACRIFICE

When studying the vision statements of organizations and individuals, it becomes apparent that real vision, in business or life, is an inspiration that goes beyond the desire for status, leisure, and money—one that serves to stretch us to be more than we ever thought we could be.

As the youngest U.S. president, John F. Kennedy portrayed the picture of health and youthful energy to the general public. Little did most of the nation know that their vibrant leader had been deathly ill for much of his life.

In fact, a priest had read the young Kennedy his last rites twice as a teenager and at age 30 he was told by his physician that he had less than one year to live. Those situations are mere glimpses into his struggles with physical infirmities. He was plagued with life-threatening setbacks from start to finish.

Many of our great leaders have had to deal with personal hardship and challenging assignments. Lincoln, Gandhi, Roosevelt, and Reagan—most all of the leaders whose lives I have studied experienced some degree of pain and sorrow beyond understanding. As a result, they were compelled to look deeply within and beyond themselves to their personal resolve and enduring faith. They found their clarifying life vision through (not "over" or "under" or "around" but "through") their trials … into lives of excellence in a world they helped to move forward.

Along the same lines, the process of vision statement development can be as challenging as its result. Defining a personal life vision is seldom easy and is without question made more difficult by the world in which we live. Our culture of "right answers" and "just in time" everything doesn't lend itself to much introspective thinking. Vision statement is usually the most thought provoking part of your plan, so don't push for a "right" answer … look for a clearing and give your self permission to listen.

When facilitating strategic planning sessions my colleagues and I ask questions to help people stop focusing on their day-to-day problems and to "think bigger." Sure, big thinkers are not always at the top of the corporate ladder, but how do you think those who got there, stay there? By asking good questions, listening to answers, and making decisions—

No true leader ever started at the top.

☐ Friends, mentors, public figures, quiet heroes who have a life vision that you want to support and carry on?

☐ If you waved a magic wand and, just by this action, one thing would change in the world, what would you want that one thing to be?

☐ What significant event has occurred in your life that you keeps saying to yourself "somebody ought to do something about that"?

TWO IMAGINARY LIVES

A few years ago I came across an excellent book with many interesting concepts and exercises to help leaders rethink productivity and learn to communicate more effectively in business and in life. The basic tool the author, Michael Gelb, uses in his process he has termed mind mapping.

The process is highly efficient means of helping people or groups organize their thoughts and ideas in a conceptual way. Our minds function in a flow of rapid connections, instead of in a linear fashion—counter to the way that we were taught our mind should work in school and in business. It is the natural, creative function of your mind when it is searching for answers or new ideas, spotlighting insights, creating new possibilities.

Below is a sample illustration of my own mapping exercise. I was asked by someone in whom I place great trust and confidence to draw a life map of two imaginary lives I was just awarded. In addition, my friend gave me the freedom to consider the possibility I could be anything I wanted to be.

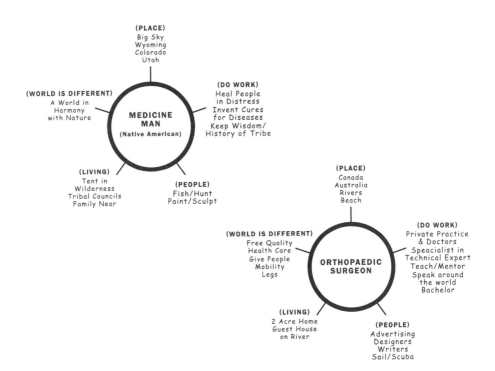

YOUR OWN LIFE MAP

In keeping with the example illustrations on the previous page, now consider creating your own free-wheeling, life-mapping sketch. Get a different view of your life vision.

Rules of The Road: You have been graciously awarded two additional lives. Each new life will last for 5-7 years each, with your second life being distinctly different from your first. You magically have all the skills necessary for any career you choose. You may live in any place geographically that you desire. No money worries either. You will have a great income no matter the work as long as you invest 50 hours a week.

In both Life #1 and Life #2 please note the type of work you would choose (inside each circle). And please note around each circle 1) the place where you would live, 2) the people you'd like to meet or work with, and, 3) how your efforts will improve the world

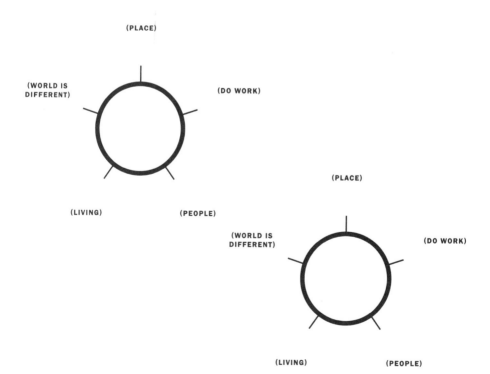

What patterns appear to stand out in your life map exercise?
Is there a common theme? What does this reveal, if
anything, to you about your life vision?

VANTAGE POINT

1. YOUR CORE PERSONAL VALUES?

Develop your thoughts here and transfer them to the section
marked **Values & Vision** on the inside of the dust jacket cover.

2. YOUR CORE COMMUNITY VISION?

Develop your thoughts here and transfer them to the section
marked **Values & Vision** on the inside of the dust jacket cover.

ONE PAGE DELIVERABLE
ADVERTISING EXECUTIVE
LEADERSHIP AND LIFE PLAN

VISION & VALUES

A world where all people to believe in possibilities and see they can overcome adversity.

People are more important than things.
My reputation and integrity are worth much more than any material possession. Everything I have is a gift from God.

CAREER MISSION

To bring creative ideas and strategies to a collaborative group of leaders, making critical decisions together that propel our team forward.

In a private work space that's well designed, aesthetically pleasing, efficient and organized; timely social interaction through business lunches, travel, entertaining home

ASSUMPTIONS

Everyone deserves the benefit of doubt, Living well is all about listening and learning. I only learn when I ask more questions than I answer.

STAKEHOLDERS

STAKEHOLDERS
God, myself, spouse, parents, extended family and in-laws, life friends, church friends, staff, co-workers company officers

GOALS
Diversify my professional pursuits.
Collaborate with world renowned creative geniuses.
Use more of my talents for profit.
Earn an income from public speaking and writing.
Give up always trying to say the right thing - embrace failure. Beautifully balance spiritual growth.
Contributing my time, talents, and resources to things that matter in the world.

OBJECTIVES

Publish 1 article per month
Book done by 2008
Become one of the top five senior executives at the firm – exceed all KPI's
Create a foundation that offers mentoring for crippled and neglected children
Retire debt-free with at least $ --million in cash, liquid commodities
Visit every state in the USA
Run a 10K or equivalent with my kids
Earn income from public speaking $ --- by Earn $ ---K annually
Give way 25% of income each year

S.W.O.T ANALYSIS

STRENGTHS

Conceptual, creative, strategic, objective, solutions-focused, smart negotiator, enthusiastic, collaborative team player

WEAKNESSES

Financial analysis, impatient, volatile temper, procrastination, perfectionism, risk averse

OPPORTUNITIES

Leadership change, industry leadership roles, community involvement, public meetings, re-engineering marketing

THREATS

Labeled "ad guy," competition for the same job(s), volatile commodity pricing, mature industry, poorly structured functional area, personal health

KEY DECISIONS

"RISK AND LIVE LARGER"
1. I will develop future two career options in the company & on outside.
2. We will visit 3 states this year
3. I will work in the leadership position at a foundation
4. I will become a truer servant leader and learn humility and patience.

KEY DECISIONS

ACTION PLAN

CAREER MISSION

2 · A Peaceful Career

[W]hen God gives any man wealth and possessions, and enables him to enjoy them, to accept his lot and be happy in his work—this is a gift of God.

Ecclesiasties 5: 19

The purpose of this chapter, *Career Mission*, is to develop a stronger sense of peace and enthusiasm about the future of your career.

VANTAGE POINT

Most people don't know what they want, but they're pretty sure they don't have it.

Alfred E. Neuman, comic book character

A musician must make music, an artist must paint, a poet must write, if he is to be ultimately at peace with himself.

Abraham Harold Maslow, psychologist

Successful careers are not planned. They develop when people are prepared for opportunities, because they know their strengths, their method of work, and what they value.

Peter Drucker, business author

In this second step, *A Peaceful Career*, you will address two dispositive questions.

1.　What is your career mission?

2.　What is your ideal work environment?

VANTAGE POINT

LET THE STRESS BEGIN ... OR END

Plastered high on the wall behind the counter at a famous pancake house was this sign "Good Morning ... Let the Stress Begin." Sadly, this is how many people begin their work day—with little desire to do what they are doing or to be where they are being. Most people in America don't have peaceful careers. They simply don't like what they do at work. A recent national survey by the Saratoga Institute showed that 70 -80% of the people in the U.S. say they "hate their job" and 50% are "looking to move in the next twelve months."

Of course, we all occasionally feel this way, and why not? We live in a world filled with potentially stressful conditions: constant change, more demands with less resources, 24/7-connection technology and more busy-work than ever just to keep things going, resulting in less time spent on the more important things in our career ... like where we're headed. All this outside chaos can drain your energy and enthusiasm, but if you want a peaceful career and are willing to invest some time re-establishing your approach, you can have one.

One's "career mission" has three parts. The career mission describes, first, what you do, and, second, the resulting benefits to key customers. For example:

> Design and plan architecture restorations ‖ to preserve
>   the essence and personality of indivual communities.

The third part to your mission is your work environment, which is the physical environment that surrounds you and which either motivates you or doesn't motivate you. So, even if the first two parts of your mission fit, you won't be as productive or satisfied unless the environment meets your needs. Some people love to work alone, some people love teams. Some people need constant feedback, others just an occasional kick in the seat of the pants. A peaceful career is experienced when you get your work done by using your natural abilities in an environment that you've designed to include the things that are most motivating to you.

This chapter is focused on tuning up your career by helping you refine your understanding of an authentic career mission, and, in the process, help you to gain a keener awareness of the environmental factors that make you most alive ... without having to take any online personality tests or go through any complicated "career inventory" exercises.

A tailored career mission in an ideal work environment. Peace.

FIRST, FIND YOUR INVISIBLE SKILLS

I have found that no matter what a person is hired to do, within a month they will have turned the job into what they naturally do best, no matter what their job description. The unfortunate thing is that people are hired and fired many times over as a result of that progression—trying to turn their job into what they do best—and they just don't get it.

They leave one job after another. Thinking they were not valuable, they lose confidence simply because they have so little personal insight into their motivated abilities and natural brilliance.

Just because a person is gifted (and we *all* are) doesn't mean he is in touch with the gifts he possesses. The things that we are best at often are invisible to us—we undervalue them because they are just so natural and easy. It seldom occurs to people to build their career, or at least fine-tune their career focus, to emphasize their natural talents and easy brilliance.

Many of us decided on a career based on the people we meet in our life. If you look back at your "Give Credit List" it will help remind you of those people who have influenced your career path in various ways and aid in clarifying your thoughts about your career mission.

Robert Greenleaf, author of *The Servant as Leader*, reminds us of the importance of studying and drawing from influential people, but cautions us to avoid the "temptation of emulation" and "pitfall of complacency." Greenleaf states, "Study [influential people] not to copy the details of their methods, but as examples of highly creative people, each of whom invented a role that was uniquely appropriate for himself as an individual, that drew heavily on his strengths and demanded little that was unnatural for him and that was right for the time and place he happened to be."

Invisible skills are those talents you are blessed with, something you do so well that you don't even recognize how good you are. We experience stress when we focus too much on the things that are changing rather than on the things that are constant. When we decide to focus on the abilities and gifts inside of us rather than allowing external circumstances to inform our behavior and choices, we are heading in the right direction to define a "peaceful career."

Whatever you focus on expands and allows you to harness your natural ability and unique perspective to your advantage. Building your career around these invisible skills need not be hard … it will be like breathing.

Imagine yourself on retreat at a cabin in the north woods, relaxing by a blazing fireplace, looking out on a winter expanse. Now is the time to ask yourself what would happen if, contrary to what the world seems to ask of you, you were to completely re-engineer your career so that you use only those skills which make you the most alive. Define and appreciate the true power of your "invisible skills," and stressful conditions will dissolve like the sleet on the cabin's window pane.

VANTAGE POINT

YOUR MISSION, NOT SOMEONE ELSE'S

In drawing up your career mission it is important to know in a definitive way who invented the career role that you are now playing. Have *you* composed your "career" in such a way that you are drawing naturally on your true gifts and abilities, or are you playing *someone else's* game? It is critical to develop an insight into the motivations behind your choices *before* you design your career mission if you are to work in the flow of your natural interests and strengths.

Should you attack this problem from your perspective as the key leader of your organization, your personal career mission will be similar, if not identical, to your organization's mission statement. If you are not at the top in your organization, ask yourself *Does my personal work mission support my organization's mission?* That's the important place to start. Without aligning yourself with the overarching direction of the organization where you work, success and satisfaction will be hard to come by.

So, here is a suggestion on finding your "invisible skills." Do not go back and attempt an inventory of your career history—a career-history inventory exercise can be helpful, undoubtedly, but only when you have days or weeks to examine your past. Now is not the time for that.

Take a moment to review the following short list of skills. Highlight the top three of these non-technical or transferable abilities that you most enjoy doing and, consequently, you do with the greatest of ease.

> **Build; organize; oversee and complete projects; get immediate and concrete results**
>
> **Persuade; promote; sell; negotiate; mediate; counsel; coach; motivate**
>
> **Develop standards & guidelines, management systems; monitor operational & quality controls; analyze; schedule activities; work with numbers and details.**
>
> **Plan; strategize; create; develop; teach; train; see the "big picture"**

When you use these abilities, the positive outcome, benefit, or added value might be one of the following: Save time–Increase knowledge of …–Save money–Enhance performance–Make money–Ensure safety–Enhance image, reputation, skills–Heal, correct, fix, cure–Improve productivity–Create a sense of …–Provide resources to meet goal or objective.

The first two questions in constructing your Career Mission
are 1) what do you do, and 2) for whom do you do it. Now
is the time to align what you do with your invisible skills,
and once you do this, you will, without doubt, benefit your
customers and those around you. What are your thoughts
about these two parts in your mission statement?

VANTAGE POINT

DO YOU REALLY CARE?

At a recent hospital seminar one of the speakers asked the question. "How are you going to do a good job if you don't like the patients?" By the stark look of surprise and disbelief on the faces of some of the physicians and other medical professionals at the meeting, after a few moments most seemed obviously relieved that it was merely a rhetorical question.

But the truth was it was not a rhetorical question. How can a doctor, a lawyer, a candlestick maker do their job with excellence and enthusiasm if they do not like the people they serve and the people they serve with. The real question however was not about "like" but about value and appreciation. Patient care requires just that: care.

I started to think about so many people who work with people they don't like. You know them—they are seldom satisfied and never enthusiastic. They are constantly making negative comments about their clients, partners, colleagues, associates, board members, and vendors. Of course, we all have low points and whine sometimes—that's just being human.

These constant complainers appear to fall into one of two categories; either they have such a weak ego that the only way they feel good is by putting people down or they simply have chosen the wrong profession and/or work environment. More often than not, the latter is the case. Misfits in careers most often occur because people follow money rather than their hearts, going for what makes them feel most alive.

One of the most successful and happiest CEOs I know (whose engineering firm posts productivity numbers and profitability that exceeds every benchmark in their industry) said "I think the key to my success has been I thoroughly enjoy the architects I work with. I think they are innovative, fun people and I am totally amazed by their creativity." He is fascinated by the people who are constantly part of his world of work. And the money follows.

Amazing how that works.

Imagine yourself in your existing career, at your same desk,
greeting your same associates, working with your same
colleagues. Your desire today, as it is everyday, is to make a
contribution and to use your skills and talents to their fullest.
You have four choices: move up, move over,
move out, don't move. Just decide ... or someone
is certain to make the decision for you.

VANTAGE POINT

A SENSE OF SUCCESS

The way we process information applies directly to our work environments as well. Your eyes, ears, hands—visual, auditory, and kinesthetic sensibilities and not just what your "heart" tells you—are the true guides to your ideal physical work space. Whether you work at home, office, plant, on the road, or some combination of these different settings, your work is an environment and can have many visual, auditory and kinesthetic elements.

There are some combinations of personal contact, physical space, equipment, rewards, sounds and feelings that inspire your thoughts and bring out your most effective personality. What do you need in your work environment to produce your best work?

Your physical surroundings at work set the tone for your work environment, but are not the only factor. What reporting structure, resources, types of responsibilities and incentives fit you best?

A young lawyer who was offered a partnership in a larger law firm came by my office last year. He wanted to develop a life plan to be sure he was making the right long-term career move. It was obvious that he loved the law field and that his specialty was in estate planning, which was exactly what he was involved in at his existing employer. So, I asked him, "Take the money factor out, what motivates you to do you best work?" He stared back at me with a blank look and said "Well, I'm not sure, but I can tell you what drives me crazy about the place." And he did.

He rattled off those issues in a matter of minutes: too much paperwork, inadequate secretarial support, no systems or procedures, reporting to a micro-manager, open office space and limited creative time. We made a quick flip chart and squared of two sections, "Drains My Energy" on the left side and "The Opposite" on the right. As a result, we had created some of the key factors that he was missing in his organizational work environment in order for it to be most motivating.

Drains My Energy	_Creates Energy (The Opposite)_
Too much paperwork	Simplified reporting/dictate
No secretarial support	Private Assistant (or shared)
Reporting to a micro-manager	Autonomy–Create a niche
Routine work	Challenging assignments
Income/Salary capped	Individualized rewards
Limited creative time	Self-determined schedule

TOO MUCH OF A GOOD THING?

What are the key elements of your most motivating and productive environment? I have discovered over my years dealing with high acheivers how easy it is for these very smart people to know what activities drain their energy. However, I have also found that they often have a tougher time in realizing and articulating "the opposite." The following is a running list of typical motivating elements in most work assignments. It is provided to aid you in your effort to spell out your most motivating work environment quickly. Choose the motivating factors that, for you, "drain energy" and that, oppositely, "create energy."

MOTIVATING FACTORS: Fast pace, plenty to do; Freedom to act, organize, implement, and control work; challenging assignments; Firm, objective supervision; Autonomy in setting and achieving goals; Individualized rewards; Variety of challenges; Clear lines of authority; Freedom from restrictions; Set polices and procedures; To know how work will be carried out and evaluated; Minimal interruptions and change; A consistent, low-key management style; To be trusted; Creative expression; Reflective time; Freedom from constant social demand; Self-determined schedule; Professional recognition/respect; A participative management style

Drains Energy   *Creates Energy (The Opposite)*

OLYMPIC RINGS OF PEACE

Five overlapping rings are a universally recognizable symbol of the Olympic Games. The rings are linked together as a symbol of hope for a world united in peace. The Olympics provides a place where the circle of every nation can link together in games where excellence prevails and world peace is the vision.

Your career, similar to the Olympic vision, albeit on a less grand scale, can also be viewed using overlapping rings. It's your choice to make—it's either a three-ring circus or it's three rings of peace. Only you can make the call.

By way of example, here is my personal work mission, followed by a written description of my maximized motivating environment:

> "To create compelling experiences ‖ where smart people get wisdom they need to live and lead with excellence."

My motivating physical environment has open rooms, stand up desks, story boards, and outdoor view.   The best organizational environment for me is in a small professional office with a few smart professional people, strong administrative support, total autonomy, time alone, limited travel and unlimited earning potential.

My individual model of three circles of career peace looks like this:

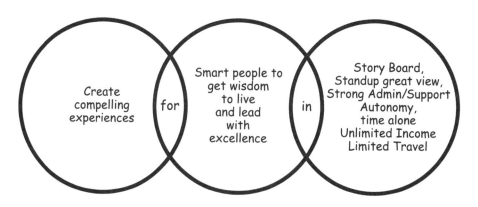

YOUR THREE RINGS

Ideally, what do your three circles look like? Remember, all your three circles need to address are the three elements to your career mission:
1. What do you (really like to) do?
2. Who do you (most want to) do it for?, and,
3. Where are you (most) productive?

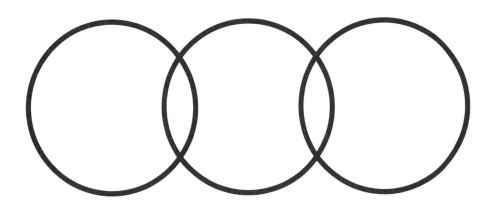

The first circle emphasizes your natural talents—your career brilliance, your "invisible skills." The second circle emphasizes your contribution—the benefits of your work efforts to others. The third circle emphasizes your ideal, most productive work environment—the physical surroundings and organizational structure in which you excel. When all three circles are linked together there you will find peace and excellence in your career

1. YOUR CAREER MISSION?

Develop your thoughts here and transfer them to the section
marked **Career Mission** on the inside of the dust jacket cover.

2.   MOST PRODUCTIVE WORK ENVIRONMENT?

Develop your thoughts here and transfer them to the section
marked **Career Mission** on the inside of the dust jacket cover.

ONE PAGE DELIVERABLE
HUMAN RESOURCE MANAGER
LEADERSHIP AND LIFE PLAN

VISION & VALUES

I will make a difference in the lives of children who suffer from abuse or hunger.

- Integrity
- Honesty
- Faith in God
- Kindness
- Family
- Respect

CAREER MISSION

I will ensure a work environment which recruits and retains the best employees

- Orderly
- Supportive
- Results oriented
- Recognition
- Independent
- Innovative

ASSUMPTIONS

- Effective Team are not about the team but about of competent accountable individuals
- Respect is built on trust which is build on keeping your word.
- Innovation is the secret to success
- There is a season for everything- timing matters

STAKEHOLDERS

Leadership- Develop world-class leadership development program/ develop and maintain succession plan that ensures a continuum of leadership

- **People Services Lead Team**- Create benchmark department

- **Associates**- Create a work environment where associates are happy to come to work and satisfied when they leave work

- **Freddy** - Continue the adventure/ nurture and support relationship to help each achieve their dreams

- **Family**- Have a family reunion with all children at least once each year

- **Friends**-Make time for friends each week
- **Church**- Develop a spiritual life that includes regular worship

- **Board of Directors**- Ensure that People Services is recognized as a driving force in meeting the mission and vision of the organization

OBJECTIVES

- Achieve employer of choice recognition
- Serve on Economic Development board
- Achieve additional professional certification
- Retire comfortably at 62
- Maintain excellent health
- Key role in child organization

S.W.O.T ANALYSIS

STRENGTHS

- Knowledge- Expert HR systems
- Intelligence
- Interpersonal skills
- Responsible/ dependable
- Conflict resolution
- Problem solver

WEAKNESSES

- Too Detail oriented
- Too self- controlled
- Holding team accountable
- Delegation

OPPORTUNITIES

- Professional development opportunities
- Increasing strategic role of HR
- Workforce development initiatives
- "Best Companies to Work " application
- Employer of choice initiative

THREATS

- New CEO
- Deceasing financial resources
- Increasing competition for manpower
- Parent's declining health
- Increasing compensation and benefits expense

KEY DECISIONS

Word for Year:

Facilitate the CEO transition to ensure a positive outcome for the organization – Read The Last Word of Power, Story Factor, and How to Put Power in Your Voice/ Research organizational transition process/ identify human resource's and my role in transition, (what is possible?)

Department structure/ support- Reassign front desk responsibilities/ secure executive assistant FTE

Balance personal goals –Regular exercise routine/ oral autobiography with mother

VALUES & VISION
CAREER MISSION

ASSUMPTIONS
STAKEHOLDERS

OBJECTIVES
S.W.O.T.

KEY DECISIONS

ACTION PLAN

ASSUMPTIONS

3 • Keys I Haven't Lost Yet

Of making many books there is no end,
and much study wearies the body.

Ecclesiastes 12:12

The purpose of this chapter, *Assumptions*, is to frame a clear understanding of the key assumptions you make and how they influence the way you manage and lead today.

VANTAGE POINT

*The true test of a first-rate mind is the ability
to hold two contradictory ideas at the same time.*

F. Scott Fitzgerald, novelist

*The only thing that separates any one of us from excellence
is fear, and the opposite of fear is faith ... I am careful not
to confuse excellence with perfection. Excellence I can reach
for, perfection is God's business.*

Michael J. Fox, actor

There is no education like adversity.

Benjamin Disraeli, statesman

In this third step, *Keys I Haven't Lost Yet*, you will address two dispositive questions.

1. What are the three most important things you know about managing with excellence?

2. What are the three most important things you know about leading with excellence?

VANTAGE POINT

FINDING YOUR OWN KEYS

I have a habit of losing things quite often, so, it has come as quite a surprise to my wife and others who know me well that I've held on to a particular key ring through the ownership life-cycle of two vehicles—for over 7 years! You see, I've had trouble keeping up with these types of things all my life, usually because I get in a hurry, try to do too many things at once, and end up not paying close enough attention to what's going on and where things are going in the process.

That fact that I haven't lost my keys for over seven years has been one heck of an accomplishment for me. That knowledge has become, as they say on the coffee commercials, one of life's simple pleasures. Frankly, I attribute much of this success to the words "The Keys I Haven't Lost Yet," which are printed in bold black letters on the tag of the key ring for my Toyota 4Runner.

Before I got this key ring, I would frequently lose my keys and the obvious next step was for me to ask anyone around "Have you seen my keys?" Then came the most common and counter-productive of the typical responses, "So, where do you think you lost them?" That's a winner, isn't it—they may as well just flat-out have asked me, "Have you seen your keys ... you dummy!?"

A more helpful response was, "Where was the last place you remember having them?" At least that's a step in the right direction ... many a set of keys has been found after one takes a moment to review their last few steps.

Not surprisingly, a response I never heard was, "Hey, here are the keys to my vehicle. Why not just use them." Why not?! ... well, the answer is, of course, obvious. Their keys won't work in my vehicle; my keys won't work in their vehicle. I have my own keys. They have their own keys.

Assumptions are our "keys." They are statements of what we currently assume to be true about how to manage limited resources effectively and how to lead people to high performance at work. These are our career operating principles or statements of our individual leadership philosophy. Our assumptions are foundational for making everyday work decisions as well as long-term work related plans. When our assumptions change our actions change.

Do you know where your management keys are? How likely is it that someone else's leadership keys will work for you?

THE BUSINESS OF SIMPLICITY

A few months ago I heard a CEO speak to a group of his managers about the tendency to complicate things and the value of keeping the business simple. To make his point, he shared some of his personal history. He told the group that as he grew up he did much traveling with his father, a savvy business man who made deals all around the country. They would go from place to place, father speaking and son listening, deal after deal. After each business meeting his father would ask, "Well son, what did you learn?" They would then discuss and share stories, both learning as they went.

He told of one particular business meeting that he attended with his father, the client being a banker who smoked a pipe. During the meeting the banker and his father discussed financing options, marketplace changes, and economic concerns. Throughout the discussion the banker seemed very occupied with his pipe—packing, smoking, cleaning, and relentlessly adjusting.

The son watched and listened as his father worked his way through the conversation, won the negotiation, shook hands, and closed the deal. When they got back in the car, the father asked him, "Son, what did you learn?"

The son started talking about the related investment rates, marketplace changes, and various distribution complications in the business. He went on for awhile, dead-on in his assessment of the details. Then his father stopped him and said smilingly, "Son, you missed the point. What you should have learned is to never hire a man who smokes a pipe. He already has a full-time job."

Management command often requires a very deep simplicity. And, of course, once a manager has mastered the skill of reducing complex human behavior to clarified impressions of fact—in words and images that resonate with his audience—there is always the risk that his assumptions will be written off as trite or shallow ... But, not to worry, as Harry Truman once said, "When the fish are biting, even the biggest problems are forgotten."

Parents, mentors, ministers, and managers gift us with many wise sayings and ideas that anchor firm in our hearts and minds—favorite quotes, sayings, or scripture that serve as reminders of the important things we know, about the assumptions we make. What words or sayings from significant people in your life have you heard that still stick with you?

If you can't find your keys, you're not likely to get the kids
to school on time! Manage yourself and the management of
others comes easy. Ask yourself wheter the "Keys You Haven't
Lost Yet"—the vital information about yourself and your
interaction with others, facts you've known all your life—still
drive your career mission?

VANTAGE POINT

THE READING OF MANY BOOKS

After consulting with many individuals, attempting to help them find and hold on to their own keys, I can't even count how many times I've had to urge clients to avoid the tendency to adopt today's mass market leaders' off-the-shelf, one-size-fits-all principles as their personal approach to leadership. After all, you're not here to start another's vehicle, you're here to start your own. You have your own set of keys—keys you haven't lost yet—your own leadership assumptions.

Please be clear that I believe—strongly believe—in the importance of life-long learning. Being educated and well-versed in many different areas through reading is important. But more important, perhaps, is the pressing need for adults to stop using education as a calling card and start using education as a tool to help them think and lead for themselves—we need leaders who are interested more in discovering their own identity and unique voice and not so concerned about knowing the latest buzz words in order to "conversationally assimilate with their peers."

I think the one real reason our nation may experience such distorted corporate governance and leadership problems is because as a culture we have become hooked on quick-and-easy management and cookie-cutter self-improvement fads. There is a swelling in the ranks of the management pundits and the history experts on the radio and the television—rewarded handsomely as gurus of a new and improved mindset. "Use my keys," they say. "My assumptions are guaranteed to work for you. Content not context is important."

If you've been in business very long, you know there is seldom one right answer to any complex question; there are countless good ideas and concepts. So many of the inappropriate policies and unethical practices that take us by surprise are the result of this guru-leadership style—a manager-in-the-making somewhere decides to lean on a book of "right answers," implementing them in the wrong context at the wrong time to ill effect.

I urge you to "look inside yourself" to review your own history of experience and you'll find not the "right answers" but the "correct ones." Step back, ask good questions about your situation, reach your own conclusions based on your values and vision and your personal career mission. Take the time and muster the courage to define your leadership guidelines—and you'll have found *The Keys You Haven't Lost Yet.*

Look inside yourself. What answers do you already have
that offer sound and serviceable assumptions to
guide you in your career mission?

VANTAGE POINT

OUR COLLECTIVE PAST

The Center for Creative Leadership, in Greensboro, South Carolina, is an international think tank whose purpose is to advance leadership development. One of their projects, the Benchmarks® study, has been to identify the key lessons managers need to learn to become leaders and determine the best environment for learning those important leadership lessons.

In their latest Benchmarks® study, CCL's *Lessons of a Diverse Workforce*, a continuation of their *Lessons of Experience* research, 1999, the Center asked a diverse group of male and female executives what events stood out in their personal life history which most impacted their growth as a leader and what did each learn from those events which still impacts the way they lead today. The study identified 16 factors of success that effective leaders need to master and 5 derailment factors that need to be minimized, managed, or avoided in a career. The report also identified the most potent experiences for learning vital lessons of leadership.

In the chart below, you can see the breakdown of experience by type of event with the corresponding impact by gender:

Powerful Learning Event	Women	Men
Challenging Assignments	14%	32%
Hardships	38%	33%
Other People	30%	19%
Other Events{Courses/Books, e.g.]	18%	17%

1.) Which challenges, hardships, or significant people have most impacted your path to becoming a leader?

2.) What lessons did you learn from those events or people which you still use today?

In the military, a new commanding officer will distribute to
the troops at his assigned base, prior to his arrival, a letter
laying out his leadership and management philosophy as well
as what will be deemed acceptable and unacceptable behavior
under his command. If you were asked to write your "letter to
the troops" as part of a new work assignment, what three main
points would you include?

VANTAGE POINT

1. KEYS FOR MANAGING WITH EXCELLENCE?

Develop your thoughts here and transfer them to the section marked **Assumptions** on the inside of the dust jacket cover.

2.   KEYS FOR LEADING WITH EXCELLENCE?

Develop your thoughts here and transfer them to the section
marked **Assumptions** on the inside of the dust jacket cover.

ONE PAGE DELIVERABLE
PHYSICIAN
LEADERSHIP AND LIFE PLAN

VISION & VALUES

Setting the stage for God's healing power to work

- Compassion
- Tolerance
- Charity
- Extra effort

South near Gulf of Mexico, Healthy active city, diverse music and lots of space.

CAREER MISSION

To establish a system and structure that make it easier to do the right thing than not, so patients receive the best possible care. In a place where:

- Quality rules the day
- Time to think and plan
- Straight forward manager
- Team work is the norm
- Creativity is valued and rewarded

ASSUMPTIONS

- Leaders live from the pain of discipline or the pain of regret
- Die before you go into battle
- Trust your heart over your head
- If you really want to do something , you'll find a way; if your don't you'll find an excuse.

STAKEHOLDERS

Jamie – do whatever it takes to support her and create an active growing relationship

Children – help them become satisfied, mature adults thru guidance and example

Church – give back more than gotten/received

Physicians & Nurses – to be an advocate/liaison to ensure good communication flow and equality for all concerned

CEO/board – make them successful by providing current data as it related to the strategic direction of the hospital.

Direct reports – provide support without constraint so they can grow to achieve professional, personal, and organization objectives

Peers – create and maintain a network of allies and colleagues built on mutual respect and confidence

OBJECTIVES

- CEO 5 years
- CMO large hospital 3 years
- Consulting 10 years
- Condo on white sand beach 2014
- Teach/coach high school 2020
- Deacon 2012
- Golf/racquetball 2004
- Travel to: Australia, England, Norway, Greece, Argentina, Israel,

S.W.O.T ANALYSIS

STRENGTHS

- Resilience
- Accountability/decisiveness
- Delegation
- Building trust by caring for others
- Structured
- Political savvy/diplomacy
- Technical
- Vision clarity
- Action/outcomes focus

WEAKNESSES

- Self awareness/too black/white
- Display power and authority
- Accountability – too trusting
- Passion/demonstrative
- Prioritizing
- Dependable communication system to all departments

OPPORTUNITIES/ THREATS

- Empty nest 2006
- Tuition thru 2010
- President's retirement
- Executive assistant trained/ empowered to communicate to departments
- Medical Center survival next five years
- Life/work balance
- Projects: EA, neonatology, and recruitment

KEY DECISIONS

Word for year: "Grow in Integrity"

Balance life and work
"I will establish a healthy leadership and life style"

Authority/power/decisiveness
"I will project a strong executive persona who's approachable"

Conscientious Building
"I will become a master at consensus building and influencing with integrity"

VALUES & VISION
CAREER MISSION

ASSUMPTIONS
STAKEHOLDERS

OBJECTIVES
S.W.O.T.

KEY DECISIONS

ACTION PLAN

STAKEHOLDERS

4 • Bridges to Secure

*He who refreshes others will
himself be refreshed.*

Proverbs 16:3

The purpose of this chapter, *Stakeholders*, is to identify those individuals for whom you build bridges in your life and why you do so.

VANTAGE POINT

We are here on earth to do good to others.
What the others are here for, I don't know.

John Foster Hall, comedian

No man amounts to anything by himself and one can
only rise by the friendships and loyalties of those
around him, which can only be secured by
thoughtfulness and courtesy and fairness.

M. L. Joslyn, manufacturer

You cannot live a perfect day without doing something for
someone who will never be able to repay you.

John Wooden, basketball coach

In this fourth task, *Bridges to Secure*, you will address two dispositive questions.

1.   Who are the key stakeholders in your life and career?

2.   What are your goals for each stakeholder?

VANTAGE POINT

FOR WHOM DO YOU BUILD BRIDGES?

Marti was a new CFO of a large hospital. Her team—consisting of a finance controller, four accountants, and two analysts—was in the midst of wrapping up their latest "fast track" goal setting process. Their 100 day action plan was done, roles were clear, and deadlines had been set.

There was a sense of exhilaration and relief among this group of smart, technical managers, happy that the time spent hadn't dwindled into some "touchy-feely" exercise with lack of substance. The closest that the activity had come to involving emotion was when, after the plan was on the wall, each person was asked to make a request to their new leader. To do that, each person was asked to complete the sentence *Marti, in order to maintain my effectiveness on the job, I need the following from you …* and, after working through that statement, they were asked to complete another sentence aloud: *What Marti and this team can expect from me is.…*

Each person did as instructed, making their requests and commitments without any significant problems or enduring emotional trauma. After they all left the room Marti turned to me and said, "This was a great start for our team, but I need to tell you, I feel like I just married 4 men and 2 women."

We may have laughed about it at the time—but there is some truth in what she said. The commitments that you make to the stakeholders in your life, whether family, business, or community, are serious ones. If they weren't—they wouldn't be your stakeholders, right? Building relationships, like building bridges, requires a level of risk and brave dedication. The motivation for these goals runs deeper than simply checking off a task list and accomplishes far more than typical goal setting. Bridges are the stuff life is made of.

"Stakeholders" is the term used to refer to the people, groups, or organizations who hold a stake in your success and satisfaction in life and work. These are the people for whom you build bridges in your life. You strive to aid them and improve your relationship with these people and organizations. You will make *significant sacrifices* for these selected stakeholders and invest in each one. Stakeholders include family, career, community, and, let's not forget, yourself.

Goals are written in recognition of, and in relation to each stakeholder. Goals are promises that state how and why you intend to improve each stakeholder's condition and your relationship with them. A goal is enduring—not directly controlled or influenced by time considerations.

A BRIDGE OF HIS OWN

My grandfather was a coal miner for most of his life. A private man who worked in very difficult conditions for modest pay, he seldom complained; instead he had a zeal for life, hard work, and hard play. Those fortunate enough to have encountered his tender heart were met with a boundless spirit of generosity. Veiled beneath a rough and rouged exterior dwelt a heart full of compassion known only by deeds.

After his passing, my mother was going through some of his belongings. On the cherry lamp table that sat within an arms stretch of his worn-out reclining chair, she found a few unsmoked cigars, his reading glasses, and a tattered Bible. While she was leafing through some of his scribbled notes, a tobacco-stained paper fell out and floated to the floor. On that faded yellowed paper was a poem called "The Bridge Builder."

It would be years later, when I was preparing a speech to be given to a group of college administrators about who their "customers" were, before my mother would tell me about that poem. What she told me affected me deeply, so I took the chance of reading it to that august body of learned educators. They loved it! I didn't let on, of course, that my grandfather had copied it years ago from a recording by a gifted young storyteller named Andy Griffith, but I also feel compelled to add, however, that I felt absolutely no need to do so since most of the big questions in life are answered to my complete satisfaction in the town of Mayberry.

My grandfather must've been very good at building bridges. My mother, Constance, teaches literacy and takes food and clothes to folks around town who may be in need. And I can testify that she has never once uttered a bad word about anyone. And, I, too, am a beneficiary. Let me share a simple story of how a mother secured a bridge for her son.

One Saturday morning, when a little boy was 10 years old, he was in the den watching Bugs Bunny. As soon as it ended, he turned the channel for another cartoon when his mother came in. "Son, you're going to spend the next 30 minutes watching a TV program that you'll forget by tomorrow. How would you like to do something for the next 30 minutes that you'll remember for the rest of your life?" Together they went to the window that looked out onto the back yard of their elderly neighbor. His mother said, "Now, Mrs. Carter is gone to the store for about an hour. Why don't you see if you can slip out and rake those leaves before she gets back? I bet she'll never even know who did it!" Mrs. Carter never found out and forty-two years later, that little boy still remembers.

The Bridge Builder
by Will Allen Dromgoole

An old man going on a lone highway
Came at the evening, cold and gray
To a chasm vast and wide and steep,
With waters rolling cold and deep.

The old man crossed in the twilight dim,
The sullen stream had no fears for him;
But he turned when safe on the other side,
And built a bridge to span the tide.

"Old man," said a fellow pilgrim near
"You are wasting your strength with building here,
Your journey will end with the ending day,
You never again will pass this way.
You've crossed the chasm, deep and wide,
Why build you this bridge at eventide?"

The builder lifted his old gray head.
"Good friend, in the path I have come," he said,
"There followed after me today
A youth whose feet must pass this way.
The chasm that was as naught to me
To that fair-haired youth may a pitfall be;
He, too, must cross in the twilight dim—

"Good friend, I am building this bridge for him."

VANTAGE POINT

THE QUESTION BEHIND THE QUESTION

Where are the orders? These words were printed in bold letters on a small brown-and-gold plaque which for years had sat on the desk of the president of a successful mercantile wholesaler. This small plaque served as a prominent greeting for every salesperson and employee who entered his office.

Written sales orders are the life blood of any organization, but they are especially vital for importers who typically have only a three-month selling season to move the merchandise out of the warehouse to make room for the next season's goods. And although "Where are the orders?" was the question that kept the main business objective at the top of the mind of all his salespeople, this business owner, a veteran who had been a traveling salesman for years himself, knew there was a more important question. Asking that more important question had helped him to build and maintain his relationships with his people and motivate them to reach their quotas and make the company profitable for many years. This other question he only asked in private to each of his sales people. Most of the time, it seemed like a whisper. "What can I do to help you make more money?"

The president knew his sales people well and he knew their goals in life and he wanted to help them reach those goals. And, more important, they knew it. He was committed to each one's success and he showed these vital stakeholders just how committed he was by asking that one simple question. So, the question behind the question on his desk became the success of his business. The question "Where are the orders?" was for the life of his business. The more important question "What can I do to help you make more money?" was for the business of their lives.

Once he had his arms around his stakeholders' goals, whether it was a new home, a new car, medical bills, a family vacation, a college fund, or a nest egg –his goal, or you might call it his "intention," became clear and he summed it up as follows: "to provide the products, support, and motivational environment—to build a bridge—so my sales people can reach their dreams." All from a simple question that in truth represented far more than the sum of its parts.

Build bridges for others and improve relationships in a concrete way. When it comes to building bridges, it's never about you ... actions taken to secure relationships are always for the benefit of those who desire to cross the bridges you create.

DRAWING ON RELATIONSHIPS

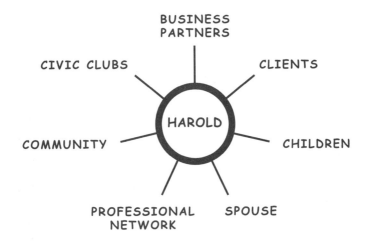

Spouse—*Strong relationship with my spouse, the feeling of dating alive.*

Children—*Be the best example, teacher of character for my kids.*

Clients—*Improve presentation skills; offer highest quality, profitable product.*

Business Partners—*Improve communications; develop feedback apparatus.*

Civic Clubs—*Organize procedures to stay connected, expand friendships.*

Community—*Increase contributions of my talents, time, and treasure.*

Professional Network—*Create value, maintain long-term relationships at work*

Above is a diagram of a person's stakeholders map. Each line represents a
bridge built on a commitment to help each relationship span the tide of
the good and bad times. Also, notice that this person has written a goal
statement for each stakeholder. As you look at this illustration, think of
how a visual representation of your stakeholders might look:

DRAWING ON YOUR RELATIONSHIPS

Who are your stakeholders?

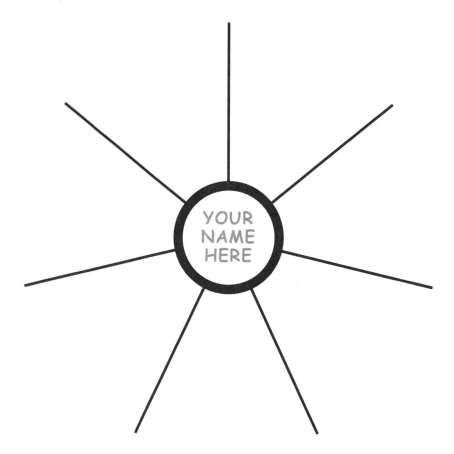

"Leave a note when you leave the house." These are the words my father said to me at my wedding, and are the secret to my parents' 50 years together in marriage. Behind these words, I believe, lies the secret to lasting relationships—create tangible lines of open communcation and concrete expressions of caring and concern about those you love. What are you trying to do with each stakeholder in your life? Defining your true intentions with these individuals is the real heart of the goal-setting enterprise. And, when you do, don't forget to leave a note!

Notes on the refrigerator
In a world without cell phones:
Messages within messages.

Gone to the ball park, back at four
—Message: "You are always on my mind."

Don't forget to pick up the kids
Message: "Thank you for teaching our kids to keep promises."

They called. Ted is in the hospital. Please hurry!
Message: "The most important things are not things."

Good News! Call Mr. Jacobs ... you got the job!
Message: "I am committed to your success."

If you could write a note to each of the stakeholders in your
life and place it on their refrigerator, what message
would you leave to keep the bridges secure?

VANTAGE POINT

DEVELOPING 'YOU' AS A STAKEHOLDER

Strong bridges can only be built by strong bridge builders. As Rumer Godden says in her autobiography, *The House with Four Rooms*, "There is a belief that a person is like a house with four rooms: a physical, a mental, an emotional, and a spiritual room. Most of us tend to live in one room most of the time, but unless we go into every room, every day, even if only to keep it aired, we are not complete."

Remember, you, too, are a "Stakeholder" in your own life. The bridge builder could not have built the bridge he built were he not in top physical and mental shape. He had to be strong enough to complete the construction and smart enough to have the tools, resources, and resolve to start and finish the job. So do you.

It is critical that you take time to invest in yourself so you can offer reliable support to your stakeholders. Just as Rumer Godden writes in her autobiography, there are, indeed, four general areas that require your vigilant attention to achieve balance in your life. The following are examples of some personal stakeholder goals, with those areas in mind:

MENTAL
(Learning)
Continue out of box thinking education and stay on top of latest trends and work only in value-based operations.

EMOTIONAL
(Support)
To go the second mile to stay connected to my family and close friends and make time to help the needy.

PHYSICAL
(Health/Wealth)
Achieve financial strength in order to give more of my income to important causes. Stay active with regular exercises, eat right and keep my legs moving.

SPIRITUAL
(Faith)
Establish an ongoing spiritual growth process each day with myself and a regular time of study with spiritual people.

WITHIN YOUR FOUR ROOMS

Examine these four ares in your life and write your goals within your four rooms. Picture a typical day in your life, how much time do you currently spend in each room in hours and/or minutes each day? Write that number in each room. How much time do you want to spend (not should) in each room? Write a statement reflecting what you are doing or need to do more of in each room each day. Write out your goals, your commitments to yourself in each room—

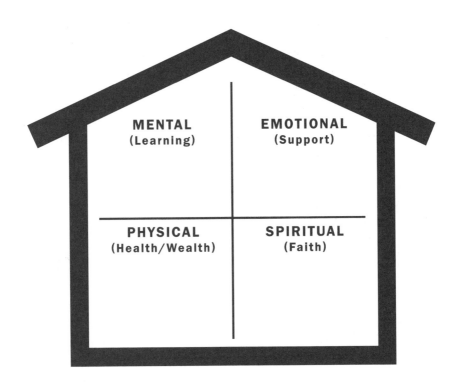

MENTAL (Learning)	**EMOTIONAL** (Support)
PHYSICAL (Health/Wealth)	**SPIRITUAL** (Faith)

Oftentimes a person finds that a single statement can meet as a goal statement for several, if not all, of the four rooms. An example is someone who wrote his personal goal by paraphrasing Ben Franklin—"To be extremely Healthy, exceedingly Wealthy, and extraordinarlly Wise." Goal writing follows the planning principle of "less is more." The shorter, the better ... and, in this case, the wording need only to make sense to you.

1. KEY STAKEHOLDERS IN LIFE AND CAREER?

Develop your thoughts here and transfer them to the section marked **Stakeholders** on the inside of the dust jacket cover.

2. YOUR GOALS FOR EACH STAKEHOLDER?

Develop your thoughts here and transfer them to the section
marked **Stakeholders** on the inside of the dust jacket cover.

ONE PAGE DELIVERABLE
POLITICALLY ACTIVE CORPORATE OFFICER
LEADERSHIP AND LIFE PLAN

VISION & VALUES

"A country where what we have is more important than what I have."
Resurrect the Spirit of Patriotism in young people.

- Integrity and honest
- Make tough decisions
- Care about others more than self
- Trustworthy

CAREER MISSION

Serve as a catalyst to help managers see workplace as place to be more than they are and leap into a leadership.

Time alone to plan; Strong support system: personal assistant and administrative operations back office; Connected to large organization Persuade and influence others

ASSUMPTIONS

- A non-human God created me and the world and loves me with a love beyond comprehension
- Confidence will carry the day
- I can't motivate a person long-term. Intrinsic love for work makes someone productive. Your pleasure is your treasure.

- Production is the truth at work. Face time means nothing- results are it.
- Liberate people to reach beyond their potential. Kind words-affirmation
- 3 things: Intrinsic spark, /opportunity , tools= leadership
- You don't become a leader you become yourself
- The business of life is the life of your business
- People try to dictate "should" you-you have a choice
- Leaders are born and then made by their decisions

STAKEHOLDERS

Peggy -Produce a secure future and keep her as my best friend to share everything with

Children-Open doors so he/she can be more than they believe. "Tap Trees"- teach matters of the heart more than the matters of the pocket book- live life less fearful

Staff-Protect them from fear factors by creating and fortifying an entrepreneurial world where their creativity is valued

Division leaders- Support capitalization of efficiencies of operations to reach common goals

Boss(es)- Produce results on time-no surprises

OBJECTIVES

- Adopt Three children by 2010
- Travel to all Deserts around the world
- Hold Senate seat by 2015
- C0O - 2009
- Net worth $ 25 --- by 2015

S.W.O.T ANALYSIS

STRENGTHS

- Rally Troops
- Single-minded focus/Vision
- Hire Top Talent
- Intuition
- Home
- Career

WEAKNESSES

- Too sensitive-Intuitive lose objectiveness
- Calendar management
- SHUT down with Aggressive People
- Don't celebrate team wins

OPPORTUNITIES/ THREATS

- Last quarter's success-momentum
- Acquisition
- Revamp Asia
- Australian Alliance
- 90 day mentality
- Adoption
- New birth child

KEY DECISIONS

Word for year: "Erase your fear"

I will "die before going into battle" at with new projects and initiatives for self and my staff."

I will lead a section of major campaign this year to learn the ropes and political lessons.

I will make may wife feel like we are dating again and my son become a spiritual warrior.

VALUES & VISION
CAREER MISSION

ASSUMPTIONS
STAKEHOLDERS

OBJECTIVES
S.W.O.T.

KEY DECISIONS

ACTION PLAN

OBJECTIVES

5 • CEOs and EKGs

[L]ike a tree planted by streams of water,
which yields its fruit in season
and whose leaf does not wither.

Psalm 1:3

The purpose of this chapter, *Objectives*, is to define measurable, time-sensitive objectives that will align with the goals you recorded in the previous chapter on stakeholders.

VANTAGE POINT

*Predicting is difficult, especially when
you're talking about the future.*

Yogi Berra, baseball player

*We do not dare because things are difficult. Things are
difficult because we do not dare.*

Seneca, statesman

Work is Good, provided you do not forget to live.

Bantu proverb

In this chapter, *Objectives*, you will address two dispositive questions.

1.   What are your objectives related to your life stakeholder goals?

2.   What are your objectives related to your career and business stakeholder goals?

VANTAGE POINT

BUSINESS OF LIFE IS LIFE OF BUSINESS

The owner of one of the leading architecture firms in the nation called me about designing a plan for her organization. "I am successful in growing my business, we have a great place to work, everything is headed my way, and yet every other day I just want to quit." After a long pause, she said, "I don't need a plan for my business. I need a plan for my life."

You are probably familiar with EKG as medical term: electrocardiogram — a vital signs measurement a physician may run at your annual physical. For our purposes, however, EKGs offer a practical way to gauge the pulse of the business of your life. Our "EKGs" offer a way to measure how you are doing related to the things that are closest to your heart.

Earn objectives consist of specific targets for your personal income, wealth from investments, education degrees, training certifications, professional recognitions, key leadership positions or big career opportunities. "Earn" objectives often align with career and business goals.

Keep objectives relate to how much money you plan to save for various reasons—planning for financial security for your later years (don't forget life insurance for your family) and also strategies related to debts that you need to eliminate. "Keep" objectives are also meant to refer to things that you will keep forever, such as, for example, lasting memories. In that area think about family time, vacations, personal adventures, or time with good friends, for example. Other pertinent topics include: health and fitness, keeping your promises and in general any bridges that you want to build for others with your wise investments. "Keep" objectives often support family, community, and your "Four Room Goals."

Give objectives include such things as tithes of time and talent, donations to charities, community service, non-profit volunteering, establishing a foundation or endowment, and civic political leadership for a cause greater than yourself. "Give" objectives are often aligned with your life vision.

Objectives, by the way, state what you want to achieve and when you want to achieve them. Objectives are short term in contrast to your goals, which are not time-driven. Objectives can be measured by the minute, the hour, or the year. There is great power to a short fuse. Reaching an objective creates tangible evidence of achievement, a clear indication that you are making substantial progress toward your life values and community vision, your career mission, and your stakeholder goals.

MOTORCYCLE MEMORIES

Charlie, my seventy-something neighbor, pulled up in my driveway one Sunday afternoon and offered me a ride on his big Harley-Davidson motorcycle.

As we were winding down a country road, taking in the scenery and talking through the helmets headsets, I asked Charlie why he got into motorcycles in the first place. He pulled off the road by a quiet stream, and hung his helmet on the handlebar.

"When I turned forty," he said, "I realized that I'd invested all my time and energy in my career and very little in my children." There was a great sadness in his voice. "Sure, I went to a few ballgames, saw them get ribbons and trophies, but that was about it. They were 10 and 12 and I didn't even know them. They were slipping away fast." He nodded his head, acknowledging the pain of the memory of that awareness.

Then, after a few moments of reflection, he smiled—a great big smile—and said, "That day I decided I had one last chance to save my relationships with them, just a few more years of time at home. So, I bought a motorbike."

Now, a happy, life-altering memory animated the conversation; Charlie was alive and brilliantly young. "Every year after that I took my sons, one at a time, on long road trips wherever they wanted to go. Sometimes we went on a planned adventure but often with no certain destination at all.

"We rode the bike, camped out, saw a lot of interesting places … but most important of all," he said as his voice began to crack, "I listened to them. We shared stories, experienced adventures, learned about each other—and I got my sons back."

Charlie died of a heart attack last year, while riding his motorcycle alone. I like to think that his last thoughts were motorcycle memories— memories of his two boys and how those two wheels saved his life.

His sons will keep those memories forever, because 20 years ago Charlie set an objective to buy a motorcycle in order to reach his goal of building stronger relationships with his children.

EKG CHARTS

I have a picture in my mind of a retiring executive cleaning out his desk on his last day at work. Old and tired and balding, he slumps forward at his desk. A hollow look of uncertainty shadows his final request as a businessman. Finger on the intercom, he politely asks his secretary, "Mrs. Barker, kindly bring me my file labeled "Dreams, Hopes, & Aspirations."

When you retire or move on to the next phase of your life or your career, what will you find in your file? It's up to you. Here are some examples of another's dreams and aspirations/EKGs for each area of life—

	2 years	4 years	6 years	10 years	15+ years
Earn	150,000	250,000	275,000	300,000	325,000
Keep/Wealth	30,000	75,000	80,000	150,000	$2M
Give Away $%	7.5%	10%	10%	15%	25%

- Write a book by 2010
- Complete MBA by next year
- Summer home in British Columbia by 2012
- Vacation to Spain, Australia, S. Africa before retirement
- Visit every state in the Union by age 95
- Fish the 20 best streams in the world by age 70.

Always consider upgrading your objectives. For example, could you take your spouse on his/her dream vacation this year instead of in 5 years, double your wealth objectives in each period, buy the best motorcycle instead of settling for less, cut that time to your trip Greece from 3 years to 2 years, earn that degree in record time, write 3 books not just one?

Big, ambitious objectives turn life from a predicable routine to a grand experiment. Big "dreams with a date" make you get more creative, take risks, and become an inspiration to the stakeholders in your life as they reach for their dreams. Reach beyond what you ever thought was possible. Play life your way ... it will be much more fun for everyone.

FOCUS GROUP

Successful organizations set clear short- and long-term objectives: big, aggressive numbers that inevitably reflect the vision and mission of the company. Such periodic number forecasts are traditionally broken down into quarterly projections which drive the "life of the business," i.e. the sales, marketing, and administrative-related business initiatives for the given year. When we think of the term CEO, we think of the Chief Executive Officer, the big-salaried guy in the corner office. But that CEO, in fact, reports to a number of "C.E.O."s and, make no mistake about it, the big-salaried CEO must astutely consider their presence everyday.

> Customers - Growth, retention, satisfaction, profit per customer
> Employees - Retention, development, satisfaction, productivity
> Owners - Sales, profits, stock value, expense controls, market share

One of the first steps in a strategic planning process for an organization is to determine the "CEOs' perspective"—in other words, piecing together the thoughts and opinions of various Customers, Employees, and Owners at all different levels of the organization and in relation to the current state and future of the company. The benefit is a better understanding of where the company is and where they're headed at that point in time.

A few years ago, I was facilitating a focus group comprised of the warehouse employees of a major office furniture store. Sales were down and the warehouse was packed with inventory—lots of old stuff without room for the new. The warehouse crew kept artfully relocating merchandise in creative ways, but they were quickly running out of space.

As we sat discussing the situation, I asked the group what they knew about the company's sales objectives. One guy stood up and said confidently, "That's not our job, we just move the merchandise." Then an enterprising young lady raised her hand and asked, "Why can't we help sell? We know more than most about this inventory and if it doesn't sell, they won't need us around to move it anyway!" The point was well received and that focus group organized a weekend warehouse sale and sold over 60% of the old merchandise!

The group was quickly recognized for their success and now the warehouse sale, orchestrated by the warehouse staff, is an annual event that has a major impact on closing numbers ... not to mention the young lady who originally spoke up is now the warehouse manager.

FOCUS FIRST

Clearly defined objectives for your customers, employees, and owners will put more life into your business. What are the CEO key indicators and objectives in your organization upon which you can have a direct impact?

No matter your position or particular business circumstance, understanding and focusing on the key performance indicators for your company can expedite your career opportunities.

If you are focused and working effectively on the right "CEOs"—in the most productive way—you will directly effect your organization's success, ultimately resulting in a more profitable organization and a stronger career for you.

If you are giving attention to the wrong "CEOs"—or even working ineffectively on the right ones—the result will most often be the same: weak profits, a dying organization, and a dead-end career for you.

Notice, either way you very well may be "working." The difference is in the focus and in how you choose to work. The focus *always* comes first.

	2 years	3 years	5 years
Customers Growth	500	700	1000
Employee Turnover	25%	15%	10%
Owner ROI	8%	12%	16%

- The Top 100 Best Places to Work in America by 2011
- Open offices in Brazil ('09), Seattle ('11), Bangkok ('15)
- Receive national quality recognition by 2010
- New product line 2008
- Web-based customer service solution 2008

1.   OBJECTIVES FOR LIFE STAKEHOLDERS?

	2 years	4 years	6 years	10 years	15 years
Earn					
Keep/Wealth					
Give Away $ %					

-
-
-
-
-

Develop your thoughts here and transfer them to the section marked **Objectives** on the inside of the dust jacket cover.

2.   OBJECTIVES FOR CAREER STAKEHOLDERS?

	2 years	3 years	5 years

Customers
  Growth
  Retention
  Satisfaction
  Profit/Cust.			

Employees
  Retention
  Development
  Satisfaction
  Productivity			

Owners
  Sales Margins
  ROI
  Stock Value
  Expense Controls
  Market Share			

-
-
-
-
-

Develop your thoughts here and transfer them to the section
marked **Objectives** on the inside of the dust jacket cover

ONE PAGE DELIVERABLE
REAL ESTATE
LEADERSHIP AND LIFE PLAN

VISION & VALUES

Peace in the World - Honor God in my life and be a leader and role model to my family, friends and community

- Family is vital/ Trust and Honesty: tell the truth – "own up to it"/ Reliability: do what you say you'll do
- On Water/ Mtn-Seasons Warm/ School System/ Religious environment

CAREER MISSION

Lead a real estate business that is recognized for long-term customer relationships, high ethical standards, quality products and services, vision, creativity and value creation.

Big picture influence/ Feedback on performance/ Autonomy/ Time alone-small group/ Clean mission/strong boss/ Variety/ Competition/sales/ Unlimited income potential

ASSUMPTIONS

- Persistence is the key to success
- Focus on "realistic" opportunities and implement
- Never burn bridges/What comes around goes around
- Different people have different motivation factors. You have to get to know them to understand how to help them be successful.

- Get people in the right place to be successful
- Have a consistent, comprehensive set of procedures & policies that are fair. Bending the rules results in high maintenance/wasted energy
- The initial setup determines ultimate success
- Balance is key to inspiring people
- Speed is the linchpin in most transactions
- Focus on today, plan for tomorrow

STAKEHOLDERS

- Lisa – Feel like she is still my special date.
- Children – Be a positive role model and enrich their lives and support their unique talents and gifts. Create an environment of security and accessibility –monitor and insure influences are positive.
- Parents – To let them know how much I care and to communicate that to them consistently.
- Me – To have a consistent spiritual growth program and honor God in my life and be a spiritual leader of the home. Make time for physical fitness and build network of "non-work" couples that Lisa and I share time together with. Learn and grow as a leader in business knowledge and wisdom.
- Professional Associations – To be an actively involved Board member and leader in several organizations – explore new.
- Community – To give back to the community, e.g., United Way and church and become a leader.
- Staff – To communicate a corporate and local vision, clear goals and objectives and create

environment of accountability and empowerment.

- Manager – To keep him informed and develop "realistic" performance plans and then execute so he is successful.
- Corporate – Set up a proactive contact plan to leverage and capitalize on business development and professional learning opportunities.

OBJECTIVES

- Develop 3 year personal plan
- 95% occupancy by 3/04
- Buy 1 pre-leased A+ office space
- Begin 2005 focus in 9/04
- Achieve $18.6 mil NOI in 2005

	04	05	07	09	15
Earn	300 K	325 K	350 K	475 K	500 K
Save	75 K	85 K	95K	145 K	195K
Give Away	25 K	33 K	35 K	48 K	50 K

S.W.O.T ANALYSIS

STRENGTHS

- Persistence
- Sales/Do Deals
- Empower staff in field w/ Clear communication
- Market knowledge, leasing experience
- Creative/Flexible/Resourceful

WEAKNESSES

- Corporate financial and operational knowledge
- Non-confrontational – take too long to decide
- Corporate Operational knowledge
- M&A knowledge
- Over enthusiasm – not objective

OPPORTUNITIES

- Presidents opportunity business
- Corporate support for deal making
- Resources at corporate to learn business
- Team development

THREATS

- Pressure of making the numbers
- Succession plan/Staffing structure issues
- Speed of deal making and corporate process
- Constant "fine-drill" syndrome
- Divisional and multi-divisional

KEY DECISIONS

Word for year: "Value Creation"

Being a CEO
"I will see myself as a CEO and act from that vision."

Work/Family Balance
"I will build our relationship by spending one-on-one time with Lisa on a regular basis."

Staff and Team Development
"I will build the team that I have."

VALUES & VISION
CAREER MISSION

ASSUMPTIONS
STAKEHOLDERS

OBJECTIVES
S.W.O.T.

KEY DECISIONS

ACTION PLAN

S.W.O.T.

6 • The Examined Life

The pleasantness of one's friend springs from his earnest counsel.

Proverbs 27:9

The purpose of this chapter, *S.W.O.T.*, is to clarify the truth about your current situation.

VANTAGE POINT

The unexamined life is not worth living.

Socrates, philosopher

Just the facts, ma'am.

Sergeant Joe Friday, detective

*Then you will know the truth, and the truth
will set your free.*

John, apostle

In this sixth task, *The Examined Life*, you will address two dispositive questions.

1.   What is it about you that will help you achieve or prevent you from achieving your objectives?

2.   What is it about the world around you that will hinder you or support you in achieving your objectives?

VANTAGE POINT

"IT'S GOING TO MAKE MY REPUTATION!"

General George Custer may not have said these words about Little Big Horn, but Kevin Sharer, the successful CEO of Amgen, one of the world's largest biotech companies, believes Custer was probably thinking them. Sharer has a picture of the dashing young Custer just across from his desk. When asked why, he will tell you, "I thought it would be good for me to look at someone everyday who was overconfident, misjudged the odds and his own abilities, and lost everything."

In strategic business planning a current situation analysis is also known as an environmental scan—a S.W.O.T. analysis—a logical, thorough examination, internally and externally, of a person or of a business environment. There are four factors to consider in every such analysis.

Internal	Strengths, Weaknesses ("In you!")
External	Opportunities, Threats ("In the world!")

The resulting inventory provides a reasonably accurate picture of the state of a business organization per area of work or in the state of one's life as it relates to family, business, and career.

Strengths	Areas of personal expertise. Strengths and talents you possess that can be leveraged to help you achieve your objectives.
Weaknesses	Knowledge gaps, skill deficiencies, or unproductive behaviors, which, if not addressed, will prevent you from obtaining your goals and objectives.
Opportunities	Major positive external changes in situations or events that may exist now or will occur in the immediate future that, if capitalized on could expedite you reaching your objectives.
Threats	External changes, obstructions or risks that may exist now or may occur in the future which need to be avoided, minimized or managed.

A timely S.W.O.T. analysis sharpens one's judgment, allowing for risk to be measured and allocated in light of current facts. After all, whatever the outcome, success or failure, you stake your reputation on your ability to look at facts realistically.

EVERYTHING I TOUCH TURNS TO ...

John is a technical genius working in a high-profile position. John has trouble coming to grips with his strengths and weaknesses. He has no difficulty at all plowing through questions about his personal and professional goals and achievements. He has a long list of strengths that have contributed to his success. When confronted by a business coach brought in to help him face the challenges in his current role, he readily admits that top responsibilities for key current projects are not getting done. The consultant asks, "John, what are some of your weaknesses?" John seems lost in thought for a minute or two and responds assuredly, "I really can't think of any."

Assuming John was being sarcastic, the consultant laughs. Like a bull standing boldly on a railroad track staring down the oncoming train, John didn't blink an eye. "Just look at my career. I've moved up in this organization quickly. I've been promoted every few years and see no sign of that pattern changing in the least. I'm obviously a very effective leader. Everything I touch turns to gold."

I couldn't help but admire his courage, but I seriously questioned his judgment. John needed a wake-up call. He didn't have a clue about the reality of his work situation at this point in time. John's boss, the president of the company, had just finished telling the consultant, "His career is on the line if he doesn't make a dramatic change immediately."

A few days later, when John trusted that the consultant was absolutely committed to his success, the truth about how he was viewed by the president and his colleagues came out. He did, in fact, have a number of weaknesses. He was not effective in relating with people. He simply had not placed enough value on that requirement of successful leadership and, as a result, the skills he did have were being undermined by his inability (or refusal) to communicate with others. He needed to do something about this crippling issue quickly or his career was in jeopardy. John then learned the five common reasons for weaknesses—

#5	Not intelligent in relation to a given task or area.
#4	Don't like to do the given task or project.
#3	Never had opportunity to learn how to do a given task.
#2	Had a chance to learn a given task but we weren't paying attention
#1	Use great strength at the wrong time (or too forcefully), situationally transforming it into great weakness.

Imagine yourself using your greatest strength at the wrong time
or perhaps using it too much. Imagine the people who care
about you the most as they wince in pity and disbelief. Your
greatest strength has become a debilitating weakness, and they
are witness to your own undoing ... right before their very eyes.
What will you do to avoid such errors in judgment.

VANTAGE POINT

WHEN STRENGTH BECOMES WEAKNESS

Over the course of his career, John had certainly identified several key reasons for weakness in his performance, but he had unknowingly committed the most common derailment factor in career and life—he just seemed oblivious to the fact that he was too often applying his greatest strength at the wrong times and in the wrong ways. John had focused on his best natural strengths so intently that his strengths overpowered and completely eclipsed the other equally important areas in his life that needed dedicated attention.

John's key strengths? His technical expertise and his remarkable problem-solving skills. As he disciplined himself to only give attention to his strengths, John began to work almost exclusively by himself, micro-managing everything. He became known at work as an arrogant and aloof leader.

He loved to solve problems on his own so much that the team that he was responsible for leading had virtually no accomplishments that they could call their own and very little sense of progress or even involvement. His strength for hands-on problem-solving had become a weakness of disempowering the teamwork efforts of those under his command.

The reality was that there were many problems that John simply wasn't able to solve on his own. The team members realized this, but because no one felt comfortable enough with John to offer him honest feedback and because he never sought anyone's counsel, the problems persisted.

When I first mentioned the situation to him, he said, "But they had an office-wide party for me each time I was promoted!" Little did he know that the real celebration occured after he walked out the door.

So how did he get promoted? John's promotions were the result of the political sway of his mentor, a senior engineer who had hired him and made it a point to protect his career. This, too, reflects a great strength turned to a weakness. John's attention to the development of a firm and loyal relationship with only one mentor inadvertently caused him to exclude other key people from his personal development—key people critical to his long term success. He had cut the network of support he so desperately needed when things fall apart down to one individual. Unfortunately, depending on how you look at it, his mentor retired and now John's leadership style and a long trail of broken relationships caught up with him.

YOUR STRENGTHS, YOUR WEAKNESSES

Following is a list of positive characteristics that could be strengths and
what happens when they are used too much or at the wrong time. Check
or highlight any of the strengths that you possess and then look at the list
of corresponding potential weaknesses.

STRENGTHS	WEAKNESSES
_____ 1. Optimistic	_____ 1. Unrealistic
_____ 2. Modest	_____ 2. Shy
_____ 3. Supportive	_____ 3. Flattering
_____ 5. Practical	_____ 5. Unimaginative
_____ 6. Reserved	_____ 6. Cold
_____ 7. Analytical	_____ 7. Nit-picking
_____ 8. Orderly	_____ 8. Inflexible
_____ 9. Persevering	_____ 9. Stubborn
_____10. Thorough	_____10. Perfectionist
_____11. Self-Confident	_____11. Arrogant
_____12. Enterprising	_____12. Opportunistic
_____13. Ambitious	_____13. Ruthless
_____14. Persuasive	_____14. Pushy
_____15. Quick-to-Act	_____15. Rash
_____16. Imaginative	_____16. Dreamer
_____17. Competitive	_____17. Aggressive
_____18. Risk-taking	_____18. Irresponsible
_____19. Socializer	_____19. Unable to be alone
_____20. Experimenter	_____20. Aimless
_____21. Curious	_____21. Nosy
_____22. Tolerant	_____22. Uncaring
_____23. Team Player	_____23. Other-dependent

Circle or highlight any of the weaknesses that you may recognize as self-
imposed barriers to reaching your objectives.

HUMILTY COMES IN LARGE DOSES

When the business consultant told John the hard facts of how others see him, he was so devastated that he didn't show up for work for several days. Telling another person that he or she has a weakness is seldom easy. We are often programmed to refer to others' weaknesses as "developmental needs" or "personal opportunities for improvement." In our hearts, however, when we honestly take the time to look at ourselves and discover our key weaknesses, we realize that to sugarcoat the reality is simply postponing the hard truth of the devastating influence weakness has in our life. Cloistered at home, John finally came to this awareness and began to rethink his career and his life.

As is often the case, the situation at John's home was not much better than the one at work. Even though his family looked picture-perfect to the world in general, nothing could be farther from the truth. Unnoticed by most, but so obvious to the few people who knew him well, he treated his wife with little respect. But, in a manner similar to the behavior of his team members at work, she dutifully put on a happy face and went along without confronting him.

When John came home that day and angrily told his wife what he had heard from the business consultant, she finally spoke up and told him the truth. She told him that sounded "just about right," and that he treated her in much the same way. She did admire his intelligence but, more often than not, it came across as a "better than you" attitude that really hurt her feelings. His attention to detail at home was appreciated, but when it came to correcting every slight mistake that she made, it didn't come in handy. And the fact that he spent more quality time with his mentor than his family made matters even worse!

The "hard truth" is seldom what any of us expect to hear, but it is always what we need. After licking his wounds for a few weeks, John took an honest look at himself and discovered humility. Realizing how his strengths had become his weaknesses, he found a place in the company where he could make powerful technical contributions. He asked forgiveness from his wife and began seeking input—even help—from those around him. He and his wife renewed their wedding vows on their next anniversary and he actually began having fun at work, paying attention to the "people side" of leadership. It is true that because of his technical, task-oriented style, John will always have to pay close and careful attention to maintaining these new relationships; but he is heading in the right direction with great momentum and team support.

HUMILTY COMES IN LARGE DOSES

As you look at yourself, which strengths do you need to build on and which weaknesses do you need to improve so that you can reach your CEO and EKG objectives?

Strengths   **Weaknesses**

Red Sox #9, Ted Williams. A fierce competitor, a U.S. Marine, a real standup guy, a hall-of-famer who, from fall 1941 to this day, remains the last Major Leaguer to bat .400 for a season. Many fans are surprised to learn, however, that although he was at home in the batting cage, content to workout under the watchful eye of a seasoned batting coach, he seemed even more at home when asking non-coaches for their advice. It seems that in an age before cell-phones-that-take-pictures and handheld-digital-movie-cameras-on-street-corners, perhaps the best baseball player ever, Ted Williams himself, often leaned on friends, teammates, and family for feedback to improve his game. He truly wanted their impressions on his swing and stance ... on how to do his job better. Must've worked somehow, don't you think?

If you have the courage to ask and receive, to seek out candid assessments of your strengths and weakness from the best hitters in your career field (mentors, managers, peers), or from the best little-leaguers in your backyard (spouse, children, friend, parents), please go to *OnTheSamePg.com* (enter the password: *yourway)* and download the free "ask for feedback" forms—templates tailored for the stakeholders in your life to offer honest and caring advice for your continued success.

EITHER WAY, YOU'RE RIGHT

A man lived by the side of the road ... and sold hot dogs. He was hard of hearing so he had no radio. He had trouble with his eyes so he had no newspaper. But he sold good hot dogs!

He put up a sign on the highway telling how good they were. He stood by the side of the road and cried, "Hey Mister, buy a hot dog" ... and people bought. He increased his meat and bun orders and he bought a bigger stove to take care of his increased trade.

His son came home from college to help him. But then something happened!

His son said, "Father, haven't you been listening to the radio? There's a big depression on. The international situation is terrible, and the domestic situation is even worse." Whereupon the father thought, "Well, my son has been to college. He listens to the radio and reads the newspapers, so he ought to know."

So, the father cut down on the bun order, took down his advertising signs, and no longer bothered to stand on the highway to sell hot dogs. His hot dog sales fell overnight! "You were right son," the father said to the boy, "we certainly are in the middle of a great depression."

In general, a threat can be viewed as an opportunity and an opportunity can be viewed as a threat, depending on our perspective. Victor Frankl, a holocaust survivor, in his book *Man's Search for Meaning*, said, "The greatest of all human freedoms is the ability to choose your attitude in any given set of circumstances."

Smart people will often try to think ahead and will envision possible "change scenarios" to create plans that are aimed at turning potential threats into opportunities before they are caught off guard. There is, without question, something to be gained from that approach ... since change is an inevitable part of all of our lives.

By the way, I have a sweat shirt that reads, "Either way, you're right." Boy, do I get some strange looks when I wear that one! This clever play on words doesn't mean that I don't believe there are absolute principles of truth in the world. It simply means that when changes come our way, we have the ability to decide on how we will look at them and respond.

One of my business partner's favorite military sayings is, "Plans change when you meet the enemy." It's important to note, however, that if you anticipate some of the prospective changes that might be created by your "enemies and friendlies" beforehand, your reaction time is usually better. When you have done a thorough job of examining these potential changes you will find yourself *reacting* less —*proactive* planning means you are prepared as well as possible for the worst and the best in the future.

VANTAGE POINT

OPPORTUNITIES/THREATS CHECKLIST

Following is a list intended to help you start identifying possible changes in your future. Use the letters to the right of the event (H, M, or L) to rate each one of the events according to its appropriate probability of occuring in your life or work future.

Personal/Family	*Probability Level (High/Medium/Low)*		
Getting married	H	M	L
Separation or Divorce	H	M	L
Recent loss of your spouse	H	M	L
Expecting a child	H	M	L
Recent birth of a child	H	M	L
Adopting a child	H	M	L
Child entering adolescence	H	M	L
Child with special needs (disability/other)	H	M	L
Child preparing for college	H	M	L
Child going away to college	H	M	L
Child getting married	H	M	L
Empty nest	H	M	L
Special family event	H	M	L
Providing assistance to a family member	H	M	L
Concern about an aging parent	H	M	L
Concern about the health of spouse or child	H	M	L
Concern about personal health	H	M	L
Family member with a disability or serious illness	H	M	L
Family member expected to die soon	H	M	L
Entering single parenthood	H	M	L

Work/Career

Contemplating career change	H	M	L
Job promotion	H	M	L
Job loss	H	M	L
Job restructuring	H	M	L
New job training/education program	H	M	L
Starting a new business	H	M	L
Gaining or losing a business partner	H	M	L
Selling or closing a business	H	M	L
Transferring business to family member	H	M	L
Downshift/Simplify work life	H	M	L
Taking a sabbatical or leave of absence	H	M	L
Phasing into retirement	H	M	L
Full retirement from current job/career	H	M	L
Buying an existing business	H	M	L
Expanding an existing business	H	M	L

Financial/Investment

Purchasing a home	H	M	L
Relocating	H	M	L
Reconsidering investment philosophy & risk profile	H	M	L
Significant investment gain	H	M	L
Significant investment loss	H	M	L
Considering an investment opportunity	H	M	L
Receiving an inheritance or financial windfall	H	M	L

Look back over this checklist and circle the 6-7 high (H) rated items that
would be most important to consider as opportunities to capitalize on or
threats to manage around if you are to successfully achieve the objectives
you set for yourself in the last chapter.

1.   WHAT IS IT ABOUT YOU THAT MAY HELP YOU ACHIEVE OR PREVENT YOU FROM ACHIEVING YOUR OBJECTIVES?

Develop your thoughts here and transfer them to the section marked **S.W.O.T.** on the inside of the dust jacket cover.

2. WHAT IS IT ABOUT THE WORLD CHANGING AROUND YOU THAT MAY EITHER HINDER OR SUPPORT YOU IN ACHIEVING YOUR OBJECTIVES?

Develop your thoughts here and transfer them to the section marked **S.W.O.T.** on the inside of the dust jacket cover.

ONE PAGE DELIVERABLE
CONSULTING ENGINEER - MANAGING PARTNER
LEADERSHIP AND LIFE PLAN

VISION & VALUES

Hands of compassion building a way for all children to experience the hand of God.

- Integrity in Everything
- Respect for Others

Life style: university town, Cultural events, Mountains and ocean, easy access to international travel

CAREER MISSION

Build a Team that provides solutions to technical problems that create high value for clients and insure safety for the public.

- Challenge- complex problems to solve
- Small group or alone
- Fast paced and structured
- Clear rewards and personalized incentives

ASSUMPTIONS

- People are motivated by being recognized and appreciated for what they do.
- People work best in an environment that is open encouraging and accepting.
- People don't buy what they don't understand- talk the customer's language.

STAKEHOLDERS

- **Karen**- To show her she is important, loved, and appreciated and help make her dreams come true.
- **Children**- To help my children grow strong in character and conviction.
- **Extended Family**- To provide counsel, support encouragement, and role model.
- **Community**- To return to my community through hands of compassion.
- **Business Partners**- To provide mentoring to become successful consultants and business leaders.
- **Customers** - To make their problems go away through responsiveness and technical expertise.
- **Career**- To be a respected technical author and teacher recognized as an expert in my field.
- **Subs**- to establish cooperative and mutually beneficial relationships that focus on customer needs.

OBJECTIVES

- $160,000 – profitable- Mechanical
- $ 8000k by   no debt- Design
- Cash pay out $ 450k by 2009
- Teaching at college by 2014
- Travel to 100 countries by age 75
- Establish adoption agency 2017

S.W.O.T ANALYSIS

STRENGTHS

- Diverse experience, industry and consulting
- Technical Mechanical Genus
- Imagination and innovation
- Teaching and writing
- Supportive Spouse

WEAKNESSES

- Too detailed to quickly
- Too hands on
- Selling process rather than outcomes
- Listening
- Marketing skills

OPPORTUNITIES

- Commissioning
- Design Build
- ISO growth
- Big Brothers
- Homeless in South America

THREATS

- Economy downturn
- Health
- Carols mother
- New Company growing too fast

KEY DECISIONS

Word for year: "Listen Inside"

Sales Skills – "I will develop my skill in prospecting and presentation and closing.

Family /Work Balance- "I will structure my time and life to stay closer to my family at home and abroad.

College Teaching –"I will research and decide if this is makes sense for me and then detail my plans."

VALUES & VISION
CAREER MISSION

ASSUMPTIONS
STAKEHOLDERS

OBJECTIVES
S.W.O.T.

KEY DECISIONS ◄

ACTION PLAN

KEY DECISIONS

7 • Weighting and Waiting

It is not good to have zeal without knowledge,
nor to be hasty and miss the way.

Proverbs 19:2

The purpose of this chapter, *Key Decisions*, is to clarify the decisions on which you will focus for the next 360 days.

VANTAGE POINT

To know what needs to be done, and then to do it, comprises the whole philosophy of practical life.

William Osler, doctor

We succeed only as we decide in life, or in war, or in anything else, on a single overriding objective, and make all other considerations bend to that priority.

Dwight D. Eisenhower, president

You can't steal second with one foot on first.

Unknown, baseball fan

In this seventh step, *Weighting and Waiting*, you will address two dispositive questions.

1.   What is your one priority word or phrase that will be your theme for the next 365 days?

2.   What key decisions will align your actions and focus your energy on this priority word or theme?

VANTAGE POINT

NO, MAN, IT'S AN ISLAND

"I keep a running task list so I can stay focused." Bob said. "See, I have six pages of important things I am responsible for now." Bob was the business manager of a highly regarded accounting firm known for it's obsession with quality. It was not uncommon to go by this 50-person office at midnight and see lights on and people working.

Even Bob's bloodshot eyes could not dampen the delight he felt in playing a major role in making his organization run smoothly. He always had his spiral notebook with him, adding things to his list as he attended at least five meetings each day.

One day, Bob asked me to help him be more effective at work. He mentioned that the area he was interested in learning more about was—you guessed it—"time management." I urged him to make this his phrase for the next six months ... his mantra ... his call to arms ... his trumpet.

I led Bob through an exercise that presents the question, "If you were going to move to your own paradise island in six months, assuming that you had someone in line to take your place, what six projects would you want to accomplish in the next six months?" He named three projects in less than a minute and shortly completed the list with the latter three. Those six projects became his action list ... which he didn't need a spiral notebook to keep up with. Bob kept this renewed action list on an index card in his pocket.

He now uses the old spiral notebook to keep notes of his progress on the "few vital" things that matter most instead of a list of the "trivial many." He has found the time to work on the important tasks using a smaller, more focused action list, resulting in smaller rings under his eyes and a much happier family to go home to and spend time with. Bob's priority was "Calendar Management." One of his key decisions, "I will plan my calendar as if I had only six months to work and six months to be with my family."

Priority Word(s) for the year refers to the one inclusive common theme, the priority that runs through both your life and your work. The Priority Word(s) encapsulate your strategic focus for the next 365 days.

Key Decisions are statements of how you will tactically address your priority for the coming year.

A THOUSAND IDEAS

Autumn was in the air, the sun was peeking over the mountain. A trapper stepped into the forest and found a well-worn game trail. He dug a deep pit and covered it with branches. Then he headed home, imagining what he would catch in his pitfall by the close of the day.

About the time the trapper's heavy boots sounded on his back porch miles away, a fox came walking down the trail when he spied a squirrel. Stalking forward, mind racing, hunger urging him on, the fox didn't notice the branches spread across the trail … until … he plummeted. Quickly gaining composure, the fox assessed his predicament. "This pit is deep and wide. But I can get out ... I have a thousand ideas for getting out—a thousand ideas! Which one, which one should I choose?"

Time passed. The fox grew anxious. His frantic pacing created a cloud of dust. "A thousand ideas, which one should I choose? Which one?" The dust rose up through the trees above, high into the sky. A crane flying by flew down to investigate. He fell through the branches, bruised and stunned, only to come face-to-face with the fox. The fox looked at the crane. The crane looked at the fox. The fox said, "I can get out of this pit. I have a thousand ideas!" The crane, pecking the bottom of the pit, simply replied, "I have one idea."

"One idea?" retorted the fox, "You will never get out of this pit. What you need are more ideas. I have a thousand ideas!" The crane again replied matter-of-factly, "I have one idea." So it went for the rest of the day. A thousand ideas! – One idea. A thousand ideas! – One idea. Soon they grew weary and both stopped to rest. In the quiet, they heard the returning trapper's footsteps on the path.

The fox jumped up. He ran faster and faster, "A thousand ideas! A thousand ideas! Which one? Which one?" The crane looked at fox, smiled and then fell to the ground. The fox shook his head, "You silly bird, you died of fright. You needed more ideas. I have a thousand ideas." At that moment, the hunter pulled back the branches and saw the fox and the crane. "You miserable fox, you killed that beautiful crane." The hunter reached into the pit and picked up the crane by its long legs and laid it gently on the ground behind him. When he turned back to the pit to deal with the fox, the crane raised his mighty wings and flew away. As he flew away, he said, "I had one idea!"

The fox with a thousand ideas became a collar on a warm winter coat.

"All great leaders are masters of symbols and stories," writes Tom Peters, management consultant. Why? Because stories and symbols offer the most effective and memorable way to convey a "one-idea theme" to help rally the troops to focus and work together and breakdown silos within an organization.

How do you breakdown silos in your organization? When departments don't work with each other and seem to be at war, when people can't or won't talk to each other, what do you do? Experience shows that one approach to improving communication and getting your departments on the same page is to develop a 6- to 12-month unifying theme that everyone can rally around. It works in business, it works in relationships. It works in life.

VANTAGE POINT

THE VITAL FEW & THE TRIVIAL MANY

The law of the "Vital Few" is also known as Perato's principle, Junan's principle, or the 80/20 rule. Regardless of how it's referenced, the essential concept that this "rule" brings to light is that in business and in life there are only a few things that produce important results.

The general idea of this concept is that in any given group of things, few (20 percent) are vital and many (80 percent) are trivial. It suggests that 20 percent of the people own 80 percent of the wealth, 20 percent of material defects cause 80 percent of the product problems, that 80 percent of the work is done by 20 percent of the team. And so forth, and so on, and thus the world turns.

Project managers know that 20 percent of the work (the first 10 percent and the last 10 percent) consume 80 percent of your time and resources. You can apply the 80/20 rule to almost anything, from the science of management to the statistical realities of much of the physical world.

The value of the vital few for a manager is that it reminds him to focus on the 20 percent that really matters. Of all the things that you do during your day, 20 percent of your activities will produce 80 percent of your results. You need to identify and focus on those things.

When the fire drills of the day begin to sap your time, remind yourself of the 20 percent that you need to focus on. If something in the schedule has to slip, if something isn't going to get done, make sure it's not part of that vital few.

This "law of the vital few" serves as a daily reminder for you to focus 80 percent of your time and energy on the 20 percent that is truly important. Don't just "work smart." Work smart on the right things. Apply this principle to all you do, and do it wisely.

RESTATEMENTS OF THE 80/20 RULE

1. The doctrine of the vital few and the trivial many: there are only a few things that ever produce important results.

2. Most efforts do not realize their intended results.

3. It is usually too complicated and too wearisome to work out what is happening and it is also unnecessary: All you need to know is whether something is working or not and change the mix until it is; then keep the mix constant until it stops working.

4. Most good events happen because of a small minority of highly productive forces; most bad things happen because of a small minority of highly destructive forces.

5. Most activity, *en masse* or individually, is a waste of time. It will not contribute materially to desired results.

6. Strive for excellence in a few things, rather than good performance in many.

8. Only do the thing we are best at doing and enjoy most.

9. Calm down, work less, target a limited number of very valuable goals where the 80/20 principles will work for you, rather than pursuing every available opportunity.

10. Make the most of those few "lucky streaks" in your life where you are at your creative peak and the stars seem to line up to guarantee your success.

WEIGHTING FOR SUCCESS

Deciding on the one priority for the next year and then supporting it by isolating and outlining the key decisions you must focus on—the 20% of your activity required to stay true to your intentions—is vital to your success. This takes wisdom, which, for our purposes, refers to placing more "<u>Weight</u>" on one thing than another, which, in turn, may require us to "Wait" before taking action, as well.

I work with a non-profit hospital organization that was recognized as one of the top 100 hospitals in the US. One day, the administrator caught up with me to ask what, at the time, seemed like a reasonable request. "Could you help me prioritize my executive team's top ten projects for the coming year?" I agreed without hesitation. What an opportunity—to work with a successful team on a straightforward, simple project, right?

The administrator then went on. "We have a list of 100 very important projects that the staff has worked hard to determine needs to be done in the next year. With limited time and resources—we need to narrow this down." 100 projects?! ... which the staff has worked hard to determine?! The opportunity for a simple and agreeable filtering of priorities seemed highly improbable if not impossible. What was I getting into?

First things first, in the initial meeting we worked with the team in order to agree on the top five criteria by which they would rate the importance of each project. We also weighted each one of the criteria in terms of how significant each was to the overall grade of a project. That information was recorded on a flip chart to be used later and the group moved on.

Before any more analysis or categorizing was done, we simply needed to take an honest look at each "blinding glimpse of the obvious," in an attempt to eliminate at least a few of these projects. With the often-overlooked tool of common sense and forthright communication the list was cut down to 30 projects in a matter of ten minutes! Next we ran each of the 30 remaining projects through the five criteria of importance that had been established at the outset, giving each a gross project score.

The only step left was to convert those scores in relation to the agreed upon weight of each of the criteria, resulting in an "apples-to-apples" net score, oriented towards true project priority. At the bottom of the flip chart page that we had originally started with, we totaled the scores and in less than 3 hours the top ten priority projects became crystal clear to the group.

WAITING FOR WISDOM

Near the end of the hospital team meeting, we took a long break and then came back for the "gut check" before for our final decision. I asked, "Does anyone have an instinct that we don't have the best ten projects listed here?" After a few moments of conscious silence, the CFO said, "Yes, there is a vital project that I am convinced needs to make this list." She spoke with such commitment and enthusiasm that the group agreed to drop one of the other projects and move her suggestion to the final version of the top ten list .

"Waiting" on wisdom is as important as "Weighting" for success—as long as each is done with intent and purpose. Sometimes smart people can be too logical, seeking facts to a fault, failing to hear the voice inside, let alone trusting it. As leaders, it is important to look past the numbers, historical data, the survey polls, and popular opinions that provide a reasonable basis for safe moves, apparent control, and the opportunity to live in a perpetual "comfort zone."

Always believe and remember that there are actually two voices to listen to for wisdom: the one inside your head and the one inside your heart. At some point in a lifetime, it appears that smart people successfully figure out a distinction between these two voices.

At age 17, Jennifer Chandler was the gold medalist in the 3-meter springboard diving competition of the 1976 Olympic Games held in Montreal. She had a world-renowned diving coach who had been with her since her early teens. She believes in the importance of leaders to trust their instincts, even when logic, experts, and everyone else they know tells them what they "should do."

Chandler has related the story of the day her coach told her she was ready to try a very high risk dive. But she knew she wasn't ready. She had always done what her coach told her. After all, she was just a teenager and he was a seasoned professional. Why was she feeling this way? The more she questioned herself, the more convinced she became: She needed to go with the dives that she knew and perfect them. This teenage competitor stood up to her mentor and refused to work on the new dive. "Something inside me told me that it wasn't the time."

Listening to "your heart" often involves waiting. Always take some time to check your spirit before making decisions. Smart people balance the "Weight" with the "Wait" ... living and leading with excellence.

1. PRIORITY WORD(S) FOR NEXT 365 DAYS?

Following are three specific places in your journal you may want to look for your Priority Word(s) for the year—

1. S.W.O.T. Analysis—Review your negative weaknesses or threats that currently stand in the way of your success and also take into account a significant positive opportunity or a personal strength that you need to capitalize on. Is there an overarching message for you here?

2. Objectives Assessment—Is there a Give Factor in chapter one that was obviously an area that you need to invest more time into in order to move closer to your objectives?

3. Stakeholders Analysis—Look back to your stakeholder goals. Is there a goal that is due special attention or major concentration in the coming year?

Remember, your "Priority Word(s) for the Year" will suggest the big picture concept, your global theme. Taking a close look over the work you have completed thus far on your ON THE SAME PAGE PLANNER™ will help you spot trends or themes. As a matter of fact, in doing so, many people experience "a blinding glimpse of the obvious."

Develop your thoughts here and transfer them to the section marked **Key Decisions** on the inside of the dust jacket cover.

2. KEY DECISIONS FOR THIS YEAR'S PRIORITY?

If it is your tendency to *weight*—to make quick, totally logical assessments in an effort to make the right answers, right away—then why not move outside your comfort zone and just sleep on it? Your key decisions can wait til tomorrow morning.

If, on the other hand, it is your tendency to *wait*—to take a long time to consider, review, and revise "decisions" before making a "final decision"— then why not move outside your comfort zone and make that that key decision today. Right now!

Develop your thoughts here and transfer them to the section marked **Key Decisions** on the inside of the dust jacket cover.

ONE PAGE DELIVERABLE
INFORMATION SYSTEMS EXECUTIVE
LEADERSHIP AND LIFE PLAN

VISION & VALUES

"To be known as the person who changed the world into a place which exemplifies God's Joy and Compassion.
To lead people to achieve more than they ever thought possible."

Serve God
Love others as myself
Honor and respect family

Life style: Rural near city
Time for woodworking, fishing

CAREER MISSION

To design the strategy and build IT into a competitive advantage for the businesss.

Active/competition
Autonomy and variety
Detail plan/structure/ see finished product
Non confrontational social contact
Feedback – respect / appreciation
Moderate pace , time to Reflect 50%

ASSUMPTIONS

- Be> Do> Have
- Do what you love, live your values and money happens
- One hour of planning saves you 10 hours of scrap and rework

- People don't care what you know until they know that you care
- It cost to much keep high performers who don't share your values
- Nip it in the Bud
- Read the tea leaves, but read them fast

STAKEHOLDERS

- Family – Support emotionally, financially, spiritually. God-centered, open, loving environment
- Church – Support financially, service, work to make it a place of true joy and compassion
- Civic – Give back more than I receive
- Staff – To create a spirit of teamwork, accountability, and innovation.
- Board - To provide IT trends and link IT to meet the business challenge of each division.

OBJECTIVES

LEADERSHIP
- Farm State is recognized as a leader in Insurance innovator in technology by 2003.
- Define I/S Dept. KPI's and monitoring system by 4/01
- Computerworld Top 100 Places to Work
- *I/S and I/T listed as a competitive strength of Farm State*

LIFE

- Positioned for early retirement 2008.
- Nationally known Speaker 2009
- Wood working income by 04
- Patricia's dream house by May, 2003
- Begin regular scheduled physical activity with objective of 3 times/week .
- Superior Bass lake by 1/1/2005

S.W.O.T ANALYSIS

STRENGTHS

- Work ethic/lead by example
- Presentation/ speaking/ facilitatio
- Implementation- Restructuring
- Responsive and resourceful
- Broad Education/ Company knowledge
- Passionate can Rally Troops

WEAKNESSES

- Managing conflict- viewed as defensive
- Responding on feet in Board
- Assuming I must be right in public
- Staff Performance management
- Recall- Memory of details

OPPORTUNITIES

- Road Trips visit Field to learn needs
- Business Lunches
- Industry Conferences – learn Best Practices, ideas for improvement
- Early Riser – Use mornings for personal development

THREATS

- Relationships with Division Sr. VP's
- Loss of key staff
- Rapid changes in technology
- Physical health
- New division relationship

KEY DECISIONS

Word for Year: " Nobody but Myself"

Managing Confrontations and Conflict:
Peers-I will design a process to reframe my stand as a leader and not need to be right all the time. **With staff-** I will set clear expectations and define the support needed to be successful with my staff and hold them accountable.

Increase Business Knowledge:
I will become a student of each division and help them design a technology strategy to increase earnings.

Next Career Foundation
I will begin to speak as an expert in technology and leadership
I will develop the skills to produce high quality furniture for gifts.

KEY DECISIONS

ACTION PLAN ◄

ACTION PLAN

8 • Henry's Awful Mistake

Hard work brings a profit,
but mere talk leads only to poverty.

Proverbs 14:23

The purpose of this chapter, *Action Plan*, is to present a simple concept and model for taking action with deliberate speed while staying focused.

VANTAGE POINT

*You have a zero percent scoring average
on shots you don't take.*

Wayne Gretzky, athlete

*The first step to having what you really want is the
removal of everything in your environment that represents
mediocrity, removing those things that are limiting ...
surround yourself with friends who ask more of you than
you do of yourself.*

Stewart Emery, business coach

*Oh Lord, thou givest us everything
at the price of an effort.*

Leonardo da Vinci, renaissance man

This final step, *Henry's Awful Mistake*, addresses two dispositive questions:

1. What are your specific actions related to each of your
    key decisions?

2. How will you change your world to increase the
    probability of achieving your key decisions?

VANTAGE POINT

HENRY'S AWFUL MISTAKE?

One of the many pleasures in my role as grandfather is to read to my three young grandchildren. Each child always has a favorite book and wants me to read it over and over. Now, I'm not quite sure whether this repetition happens because the child likes the story so much or because there is a message which they, in their innocence, know that we adults need to remember.

One favorite story they all agree on is *Henry's Awful Mistake* by Robert M. Quakenbush. It is a comical story abou a duck named, you guessed it, Henry. Henry is preparing a meal for his friend. The doorbell rings. As Henry goes to greet his guest, he sees an ant on the wall. He swats at the ant and misses it and it takes off across the room, with Henry close behind. Henry chases the ant around the house, upending all the furniture. The ant finally runs into the pantry. Henry dives after it, throwing all the food containers out.

At long last, Henry spots the ant. He grabs an iron skillet, swings to squash the ant, and misses. The skillet goes through the wall and breaks a water pipe. The house fills up with water and is washed away, along with Henry, the ant, and his guest.

The last few pages of the book show Henry a year later with a new house and a hot meal on the table. The doorbell rings, and as Henry goes to welcome his friend, he sees an ant. The last line? " … and Henry looked the other way."

Action plans are specific action steps which describe what you will do to make your key decisions become reality. Action plans include personalized techniques and specific methods as well as a time frame for completion. They often identify key individuals who will provide support, coaching, and accountability.

Growth can produce transition and transition can produce growth, but transition usually will occur first. This is true for an organization or a person's life. Transition is self imposed and change is externally imposed, but either way, for a transition or change to achieve it's intended outcome in work or life, specific factors need to be addressed, and that's where we turn now ....

Transition & Change ... Now's the time to take action and define the steps you will take to realize your goals ... to place service above self.

THREE 'M' FACTORS FOR TRANSITION

Robert Epstein, PhD, former *Psychology Today* editor, once surveyed more than 2,000 years of self-change techniques. These techniques included most self-change methods proposed by religious leaders, philosophers, and psychologists as well as behavioral science research that began being strongly promoted to Americans in the 1960s.

Dr. Epstein concluded that there are only a dozen or so behavioral change techniques that are distinctively different. Of these techniques, his research showed three methods that deserved particular mention because they are proven to be "powerful, simple, and easy to learn." The research showed that people who have made successful transition in their lives often seemed to rely on these methods.

Dr. Epstein called these techniques "The Three M's"—

Modify Your Environment (Structure)

Rearranging your space to stimulate and reinforce new behavior.

> "To change yourself is to change your world."

Monitor Your Behavior (Systems)

Monitoring or recording what you do results in improved performance.

> "To change yourself, heighten your awareness of your behavior."

Make Commitments (Relationships)

Establish a contingency of reinforcement by committing to others.

> "To change yourself, arrange for a reward if you comply and
> punishment if you don't."

THE 3Ms IN ACTION ... WITH RESULTS

Slough Creek is a pristine ribbon of water meandering its course through a meadowed valley in a high mountain range in Wyoming. The gem-like clarity of the snow melt provides perhaps the best native cutthroat trout fishing in world—but, before you experience it you are expected to earn it. Carrying a 50-pound backpack for 10 miles is the challenge. Even, I quickly realized, a death-defying feat, perhaps, particularly if you're not in shape and also happen to be carrying an extra 25 pounds around your waist-line ... as I was three months before we were to leave.

It was at that time, during the 90-day countdown to the trip I had looked forward to for so long, that I was introduced to the Weight Watchers program—and their particular application of Dr. Epstein's three M's.

When I signed up with Weight Watchers, I made a commitment to pay for the service and agreed to weigh-in each week in order to track my progress. As part of the diet implementation, I was also asked to obsessively monitor my behavior, i.e. food intake, by writing down what I'd eaten for each and every meal.

That reporting resulted in inherent punishments and rewards since my food consumption was converted into a points-based system that determined my eating options all day, every day. As a result, I modified my environment by cleaning the cupboards of Girl Scout cookies, Krispy Kreme donuts, and other snacks, and (regrettably, at the time) replacing them with more healthy foods.

I lost 20 of those extra 25 pounds in three months by making that commitment, monitoring that behavior, and modifying that environment. I took the trip, managed to manhandle the trail hike, and had enough fuel left in the tank to enjoy the experience—a week's worth of breathtaking moments in the wilderness along with enough fishing stories to last a lifetime.

Now that you have restated your **values and** articulated your **vision**, written a **career mission**, clarified the **assumptions** you make in life, remembered your **stakeholders**, defined your **objectives**, completed a **S.W.O.T.** inventory, and have prioritized your **key decisions**—

ACT! Modify your environments, monitor your behaviors, and make your commitments.

CHANGE THE WORLD AROUND YOU

The hospital administrator we visited in the last chapter taped his team's "Top Ten Projects" list to the wall of his office and left it there for the whole year. If a member of his team came in to discuss a time constraint, budget challenge, or a workflow problem, for example, he would ask them how it related to one of the projects they had made a commitment to. If they couldn't explain how their issue aligned with the list taped to the wall, the discussion ended quickly.

He modified his team's environment with the list on the wall, monitored his team's performance by requiring specific progress status reports, and reinforced the commitment made by each individual by rewarding or punishing them as appropriate, based on their ability to stay on task.

I have had clients modify their environment by simply rearranging the furniture in their office to make it more inviting and friendly. Sometimes just closing their door for a few hours a day in an "open door policy" work world will help them get their important work done. In the home setting, I've heard of people placing their exercise bike in front of the TV screen so they can't be a couch potato.

Remember Bob, the manager of the engineering firm who was living in a world of chaos? He used the 3Ms to get control of his career and focus his time. He modified and monitored to change his behavior and achieve his objectives. He altered the size and space where he made his notes by using an index card instead of a notebook to record his tasks list. This simple downsizing was a constant reminder of the 80/20 rule—to work on the vital few rather than the trivial many. He tracked his own activity by keeping a record of his progress on each of his six targets daily. Bob used this approach in order to give an accurate account of his work at the monthly principals meeting and as a basis for punishment or reward.

Small, purposeful modifications in habit beget major shifts in lifestyle and work performance. How you approach making those modifications is based on your personal style, your environment, and your distinctive way of reasoning.

On the following pages, you will find two ways to look at this: 1) **a very structured model** and 2) **a not-so-structured model**, each of which I have used over the past 10 years in my coaching practice. Look over these examples and see if you find a part or section to be helpful as you activate and customize your own action plans based on your one-page planner.

3Ms FOR STRUCTURED THINKERS

If you like structure, detailed forms, and linear approaches in your work and life, below is an example of a structured action plan for your review.

My Key Decision (What Do I Intend to Do?) ...

...I will plan my calendar as if I had only six months to work and six months to be with my family.

Expected Outcomes (How will I know I've been successful?) ...

...When I achieve this, I'll have a sense of control –increased productivity in the office–work fewer hours–become a partner –have dates with my wife and take week long vacations with my family twice a year.

... My life and/or work stakeholders who will be impacted by this are: spouse, kids, peers, community, boss

... The difference(s) they will notice: I am a happier, funnier, less stressed, more confident and productive person who keeps his promises.

Action Steps With Dates (3Ms)

1. **Modify Your Environment**–Clean Office, Plan my day on an index card—top 5 things only (3 work-2 family)—set a schedule time.

2. **Monitor Your Behavior**–I will keep a list of all my accomplishments in my notebook after I check off the top 5 each day.

3. **Make Commitments**–I will meet with my spouse each Sunday, and with my assistant each morning and go over the top 5 and report each week on progress with the team. Find a peer at another professional service firm to meet with monthly as accountability person.

Reading/Education–How will I add to my knowledge base?

Read *Ordering your Private World* by Gordon MacDonald.

Gratitude: How will I demonstrate my gratitude to my stakeholders?
Write thank-you notes once a month to one person.

3Ms FOR THE NOT-SO-STRUCTURED

New Years resolutions seldom result in anything but a public statement of resolution, followed promptly by a private acknowledgment for an embarassing lack of resolve. Why? Because 80% of people don't take the necessary first steps towards action. Those who state their resolution yet drop out typically do so because they haven't rearranged anything in their world to support their commitment. The most basic step is a schedule forcing you to pay attention to areas that are important for a fixed percent of your time each day. This is schedule management and here's how it might work for an executive in a large organization.

Ian Percy, a world renowned management consultant and a seasoned author in leadership development, offers senior level executives the 30/30/20/20 guide for scheduling their success.

30% to "brain trust" or thinking time. Not solving problems or fixing things, but reflection, reading, researching new ideas and developing your intuition. Based on a 50-hour work week that's 15 hours—3 hours a day.

30% in communication—insuring internal and external communication. Internally creating community or what he calls "Common-unity". Do this by visiting departments and sharing news of struggles and triumphs and spreading the message that " we are one" for three hours a day". It is much the same message externally. With confidence and truth the leaders tells the customer: "We are one" to serve you.

20% of your time mentoring/succession planning. These 10 hours a week or 2 hours a day are invested in coaching and people-development— helping people do things for themselves so they grow stronger, more autonomous, more likely to become mentors and coaches to others. The goal is their advancement, not yours.

20% in operational details; measurement, spread sheets, and budgets. We must have a handle on the fiscal side and most executives have trouble limiting themselves to the 20% here. This is the stuff the CEOs and their peers talk about all the time. The reality is that effective executives have hired competent managers who keep a handle on this vital data and are adept at keeping the executive sufficiently informed and timely aware. If the executive does not hire competent managers, he is in fact a micro-manager and not an executive, and will often find himself spending up to 80% of his time in operational issues, missing the mark of leadership.

Many smart people list the excuse of "not enough time" as a weakness on their plans. Well, guess what? From the guy on the street looking for work to the presidents of companies large and small—research reveals that everyone, to a man and to a woman, still has 24 hours-a-day, 365 days-a-year. Perhaps the problem is not time. Perhaps the problem is indeed Henry's Awful Mistake?

Whether you choose the 3Ms for the structured form, the daily percentage allocation form, a rearranged schedule, a flip chart paper taped to the wall, index cards or a one-page strategic life plan, if you really desire to get what you want, you need to decide on some method, means or mode that works, or—make no mistake about it—time will decide for you.

What will you do to make sure you "look the other way," keeping your eyes on your dream, when the ants try to take you down a river of indecision? Smart people know that success is not determined by how smart you are; it is determined by the decisions that you make ... and the actions that you take.

VANTAGE POINT

1. WHAT SPECIFIC ACTIONS DO YOU COMMIT TO THAT ARE RELATED TO EACH OF YOUR KEY DECISIONS?

Develop your thoughts here and visit www.OnTheSamePage. net to find a 3M Action Plan that you can use as a template.

2. HOW WILL YOU CHANGE YOUR WORLD TO INCREASE THE PROBABILITY OF ACHIEVING YOUR KEY DECISIONS?

Develop your thoughts here and visit www.OnTheSamePage. net to find a 3M Action Plan that you can use as a template.

ONE PAGE DELIVERABLE
LAWYER
LEADERSHIP AND LIFE PLAN

VISION & VALUES

Business ideas become realities for many good people

- Moral virtue
- Hard work
- Forthrightness

CAREER MISSION

Develop a highly effective practice team to create world class public/ private partnerships

- Autonomy/ ample time to think through
- Involve in "cutting edge" concepts
- Put puzzle pieces together
- Clear mission/ objectives/ measure success
- Friendly supportive partner/ boss

ASSUMPTIONS

- Exercise your ability to choose
- He who serves well/ profits well
- Frugal with money, make it for you
- Excellence in everything
- Life long learning- continue education
- Delete had habit and replace quickly w/ good habit

STAKEHOLDERS

- **Spouse**- Create a feeling of romance and strength

- **Kids**- Teach life values by my life example/ invest in play time/ model acts of service

- **Clients**- Provide excellent work in a timely efficient manner

- **Community**- Focus on building business and community service will come as it will

- **Me**- Be a spiritual person as a father and husband and find the right balance to make my life and family the best in each seasons

- **Support Staff**- To encourage and reward the development of systems and processes to free me up and increase staff billing time

- **Top Level**- To build stronger business relationships through understanding their needs and keeping them up-to-date on my future plans

- **Clients-Referral Attorneys**-To build selected relationships on a personal basis, actively capitalize on referral opportunities

OBJECTIVES

	02	03	04
Total Billing	800K	1M	1.5M
Real estate	125K	200K	250K
Knowledge	125K	200K	250K
Employment	150K	250K	350K
Healthcare	150K	175K	205K

S.W.O.T ANALYSIS

STRENGTHS

- Likeable/ put people at ease
- Competent/ expert in my field
- Sales/ entrepreneurial bent
- Relationship building
- Legal experience
- Innovative, intuitive, judgment
- Good with numbers

WEAKNESSES

- Burdened with details- not follow through/ worry
- Trouble concentrate on task at hand/ too many ideas
- Can be too unconventional and avoid formal control/ structure

OPPORTUNITIES

- Virtual office
- Hire executive assistant
- Seminars with spouse
- Regional development
- American Bar Association

THREATS

- Staff overloaded- turnover
- Family time limited
- Spouse wants to keep up with the Jones's
- Relationship with partners/ firm approval of my vision
- Someone taking your market niche

KEY DECISIONS

"Fluidity of life and work"

Over Controlling/ Delegating – I will change my environment to be more hands off and utilize my resources smarter

Family First- I will demonstrate my commitment to my family. Strengthen connection w/ spouse and kids

ACTION IS NOW REQUIRED

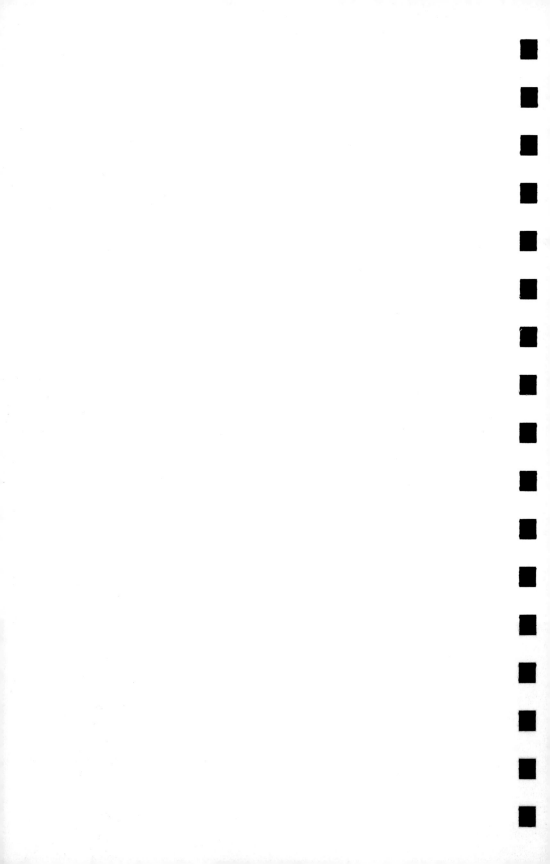

AFTERWORD

Why Faith & God Matter

How much better to get wisdom than gold,
to choose understanding rather than silver!

Proverbs 16:16

The purpose of this *Afterword* is to introduce ideas on matters of faith and the concept of an individual's soul, a very personal expression of my belief in the absolute importance of every person's relationship with their creator.

VANTAGE POINT

To be nobody but yourself in a world that is doing it's best, night and day, to make you just like everybody else, means to fight the greatest battle there is and to never stop fighting.

e.e. cummings, poet

Not much happens without a dream.
And for something great to happen,
there must be a great dream.

Robert K. Greenleaf, essayist

What decisions have you made that can only
be explained by your faith in God?

SATURDAY NIGHT FERVOR?

Several years ago there was a "Saturday Night Live" news report about an evangelical Christian couple who had founded a faith-based TV program. This couple went on to build an extravagant retreat and life center and were shortly thereafter involved in a scandal that robbed many people of their money and confidence in Christian leadership. The public disgrace concluded with the trial and imprisonment of one of the founders. During the trial an SNL news correspondent said she had tried several times to get interviews from the staff. However, after being declined by all, she was most fortunate to have landed an interview with God Himself. She mentioned that God seemed rather busy and that he only had one thing to say. *I don't know who these people are. I don't understand what they are doing, but I wish they would stop using my name.*

Not surprisingly, faith, God, and the subject of spiritual belief almost always comes up in private conversation when I work with people on their life plans. It is always with great fear that I step onto this hallowed ground to share my perspective. Too many people over the ages have spoken their views of heavenly things with good intentions ... while paving the road to hell. I pray that my thoughts and impressions will not cause anyone to stumble in their own, individual faith journey to finding truth.

My bias? I look at the world though Christian eyeglasses. You may look at the world through other faith lenses or perhaps through lenses of no faith at all. I honor and respect your perspective. It is not my intention to replace your spectacles with mine, but it is of utmost importance for every leader to decide on the place, if any, of faith and God in life—it is my belief that real success in life and leadership requires a spiritual foundation. At the very core of every true success we will find faith.

How to create a compelling experience around this vital topic while at the same time not preaching at you or attempting to give you another creed to live by? In preparation for the task, I found myself staring far too often at a blank screen ... so, I finally decided to do what I should've done first—I prayed. And since, by way of admission, I am a business consultant, I prayed the consultant's prayer. And then I laughed. The result is a highly personal, idiosyncratic work of poetic fiction which sums up my thoughts and musings on matters of faith in the marketplace ... I hope the piece conveys my faith that God has a unique plan for each and everyone of us, if we but listen and ask the right questions.

*God, get me out of the way so that these smart
people will get what they need from You today.*

THE CONSULTANT'S PRAYER

A MASTER PLAN

IN THE BEGINNING, we were in darkness, void of physical shape or form, yet whole in being. God then appeared before us in the light and whispered, *Will you bring more beauty, more truth, more justice, or more knowledge into the world? Which do you choose?*

"I choose that one," we each said, and the Creator replied, *I really need you to become that other one ...*

Our spirits sank ... slowly we looked up and our eyes met His. With a nod and a smile, He said, *Ok, Ok, so we're both right!* We then laughed, together, the rich laugh of joy and hope, and, as the angels joined in and gave a wings-up, God, still smiling, wrote it all down.

Then the author of life looked deep in our soul and said, *I have made you brilliant in a way no one else is or will ever be. I inscribe in you unmatched gifts, distinctive talents, and genius abilities. With the ease of soft breathing you shall use these gifts in your works of creation in the world. Your eyes and ears have been tuned to draw you to those places and people of Earth where you will find your soul satisfied. When your life aligns with the master plan, you will be most alive and feel closest to me.*

We nodded in complete and contented silence, and God, yet again, wrote some more.

Now the great servant leader looked at what He had written and said, *Excellent. Go. Give. Become. Do what you are designed to do. Do it large. Live well. Love deeply. Laugh a lot. Remember, I am committed to your success. I am only a breath away. Stay in touch.*

God's voice began to fade away, and then, suddenly, just as quickly, it returned. He reappeared, and said, *Just one more thing, I almost forgot to give you your word.*

He smiled. *It's the one word I give to every child. It is the most important word that you and every human being will ever have. It is the one word that no one on Earth can give you — it can only come from me. In this one word are all your answers.*

The word is "Why."

A GREAT DREAM

Birth … then a new, different light.
We go to this new, different light and a cold world receives us.
Our eyes blink. Our minds blank.
We lose sight of God and His plan for us.
Laughter now turns to crying.
A new, different, human voice says, "Cry.
     Yes, crying is good, very good."

We want to be good, so we cry some more.
Voices we now hear are caring, but somehow
     it's a different caring.
These voices speak to our head, not to our heart.
We yearn for that original voice that spoke to our heart.
We still feel God's loving whispers in our dreams,
     cuddling us, calling us like a warm blanket.
So, we sleep a lot in these beginning Earth days,
     staying close to our creator.
God, shepherd to innocence, remains near.

Play … not for long do we sleep.
The breaking light of each new morning urges us on.
"Get Up. Go! Learn, invent, walk, run. Be what you are.
Be a creator, discover your gifts.
Use your strengths.
Be strong and full of the energy of new life."

Words … the words of Heaven are the only ones we know.
The great people laugh at our unknown tongue for a while.
Then they grow impatient and teach us the right way …
Their language, their words.

When we speak the right way they laugh and we laugh.
And we feel like we belong.
Then we remember our one divine word. "Why."
We begin to ask it all the time.

Until we learn that "Why" is not a word the great people like.
It makes them seem anxious and concerned and annoyed.
We stop asking and they nod with approval.

We learn fast. We are fitting in.
God's voice grows fainter.

Rules … As we grow, we find there are many.
There are right answers for most everything.
Everyone wants to know "How" not "Why."
How we should or ought or must do things—
just to be sure that we get it right.

Imposing teachers with many commandments shout,
"Life is hard enough without having to think.
        Why make decisions for yourself!"
Everyone nods in approval or raises their hands
        in agreement.
"Why?" we ask out loud.
"Why them? Why now? Why this way? Why not …?"

It is as if we have not spoken.
"You are only a child, don't think so much," the sages counsel.
        "Trust us. We know the way to living well—

Rules ... "Follow us," they say.
We will show you the method for missing misery and
        the secrets to finding success and happiness.

They rage with voices of thunder.
It is hard to hear anything else.
So, we ask "Why" no more.
We trust them, listen to them, love them. We do as we are told.
"Why" is only whispered ...
We learn to ask "How" instead.
Asking people "How?" makes them feel proud.
Asking "Why?" makes them think.

Soon the voices of the self-appointed, the prophets who pave
        the way, become but murmurs in our ears.
Following them hurts deeply more than it makes us laugh.
Their rules, their secrets are not working. What are
        the real answers, we ask.
Surely, some expert must have a better way
        —or at least have the right answers.
Surely, someone, somewhere down here can help?
Please make it easy for us. We don't understand.
God's voice is quieter still.

Choices ... tassels, gowns, caps in the air, applause.
They say, "Now it's time to decide. Think for yourself.
        Make a choice. Do something."

Like taking our first baby steps, we toddle around
          the city seeking someone or something to hold onto.
What is the secret to living well, being happy,
          successful, and fitting in?
A yearning inside to care, to help, to follow our heart,
          to love again.
But instead we turn back, in lockstep with the crowd.
We return to the great people.

Like a flash—the answer. It seems so obvious.
Successful people, happy people take. They don't give.
They collect, they count, they control things.
          Right. That's the answer.
If we had only paid attention to this before and had learned
          the secrets of "How." How to take, how to make more.
Take and make more money, make more career opportunities.
More stuff, yes, more. Much more.

Answers ... A stellar career. A picture-perfect spouse and family.
          A big house.
We have it all. We work hard, rediscover our talents
          and the joy of creating.
Pour our soul into the work we love, like bliss.
          We ask, "More? How do we get more?"
We remember the great humans, the experts' words,
          their books, their advice.
"Take care of ourself first—take more, take credit, take back."
We look at what we have ... and ... they are right, it's working!
Fast money, fame, success.

The spotlight's on us.
We finally let go of the "Why"—
   "why" we are doing what we are doing.
We let go of our friends, our family, our faith.
Everything in a rushing brilliant blur.
Then, just as quickly as it came, it's all gone.

Alone …
We work harder and buy more things.
It makes us laugh … until the empty fog descends.
There has to be more than this, but we have trouble
   slowing down, being still …

Straining to hear God's whispers—
His still, small voice seems so far away.
He speaks, but our ears are now tuned
   to the louder, human voices.

Wake up calls … everywhere.
   Near misses. Crisis after crisis.
Answers written in each, but we look for
   blame, not answers.
Pride silences God's voice.

Shudderings … half in this world, half in the next.
Losses, trauma, death, loved ones, finality … Why?
We yearn to go back to the light, to the original voice,
To run away from this mess we have created. Now.
But the designer of the beginning and the end whispers,

I need you to stay here a while more.

> *To remember the master plan we made.*
> *Give back much more than you take.*
> *Give credit before it is due.*
> *Give up control and trust in Me*
> *Give thanks in every step you take ...*

And, oh, yeah, thanks for using your word. It's about time.

"Why?"... awakened to the truth by this simple word.
Insight, wisdom, true wealth.
Reborn to living the life we were *designed* to live.

Still, we struggle with the creator of life. He does not
        struggle back, yet whispers, *You decide.*
We hear the original voice. We listen.
We choose another way—

> Whispers over shouts.
> Giving over taking.
> Hard answers over easy blame.

Finally, we laugh again, that deep, joyous laugh,
        and love richly once more.
Content, we create with joy. We give our gifts away
        with the ease of soft breathing.
The wisdom of Heaven applauds.

A SACRED TABLE

It's time … the original voice will say.
Return to the light.

God will be sitting at a table … a kitchen table, perhaps.
        Pull up a chair. Please, have a seat.
We will sit side-by-side with our maker and his helper.
On the table will lay open a large tattered scrapbook, the book
of our life, ragged, filled with news articles, snapshots, trophies,
awards.

We will read scribbled notes about the ups and downs,
        the struggles and triumphs of our life.
Laughing, crying, reliving all we had gained,
        all we had lost.
Then God's eyes will look deep into ours and ask, Why?

We will then blast through hell and heaven in an instant …
Back at the kitchen table and …

God … the giver of all will reach across the table and
        pick up the book of our life. Removing its dust cover,
        He will turn it over and smooth out the edges.
He then will set before us the plan that He and I had
        written together in the beginning.
Silent and still, we will read carefully and purposefully.
Then we will look up in simple delight.

God will whisper … Excellent.

ON THE SAME PAGE, AT LAST?

My commitment to you at the beginning of this process was that you
would have a unique product when you finished this book—a one-page
strategic life plan that would guide you to making wiser decisions in your
life and work. If for some reason you didn't complete the journal along
the way; I encourage you to remove the dust cover, smooth out the edges
and record your plan now.

Or you may wish to go online for more resources about life planning and
organization. (Incidentally, I've heard it said and I believe it's true that
God invented wireless communication a long, long time ago. So, it seems
reasonable to me that God surely must have a computer on His table by
now, too!) Go to the resources section of **www.OnTheSamePg.com** (the
password is *yourway*) and download additional copies of the ON THE
SAME PAGE PLANNER.™ Change or redesign it to fit your needs. The
only thing I ask of you is to please make it fit on one page. Life is short.
Let's spend the majority of time on earth living it—not planning it.

I would enjoy getting a copy of your plan when you finish it ... and
in hearing stories of how you have used it. I suggest that you consider
updating your plan each year on your birthday. High-achievers tell me
that it keeps them on their toes, excited about the annual update to
their goals and objectives. If you'd like a reminder to make sure you are
prepared, please email your birth date and I will send you a reminder as
well as ideas and suggestions for updating your plan each year.

Please send questions, comments, suggestions, and stories about your
successes and failures in implementing your plans. Share your experience
of working through this journal, positive or negative. Contact: Author@
DesignALifeBook.com.

Let me thank you again for your openness to this life-planning process, for
having the gumption to take your best shot at changing the world—while
planning, praying, and laughing along the way with the rest of us.